CHOOSING HAPPINESS

Design for Growth: Twelve Steps for Adult Children,
  Veronica Ray

A Moment to Reflect: Meditations for Codependents,
  Veronica Ray

A Moment to Reflect: Meditations on Spirituality,
  Veronica Ray

Stairway to Serenity: A Spirituality of Recovery,
  Mark L.

CHOOSING HAPPINESS

The Art of
Living Unconditionally

Veronica Ray

A Hazelden Book
HarperCollins*Publishers*

FIRST HARPERCOLLINS EDITION PUBLISHED IN 1991.

This edition is printed on acid-free paper that meets the American
National Standards Institute Z39.48 Standard.

Library of Congress Cataloging-in-Publication Data

Ray, Veronica.
    Choosing happiness : the art of living unconditionally / Veronica
Ray. — 1st HarperCollins ed.
        p.   cm.
    "A Hazelden book."
    ISBN 0–06–255356–9
    1. Happiness. 2. Conduct of life. I. Title
BJ1480.R39 1991
158—dc20   90-55300
                                                                 CIP

91   92   93   94   95   MV   10   9   8   7   6   5   4   3   2   1

CHOOSING HAPPINESS

Contents

Acknowledgments

I am very grateful for having had the experience of writing this book. I thank my editors, Rebecca Post and Judy Delaney, for all their help, encouragement, and work. I thank everyone who shared their stories and thoughts with me so I could share them with you. I thank my husband and daughter for their unconditional love, and God for *everything*.

CHAPTER ONE

Conditional Lives

*What are the "ifs" and "buts" that limit my
enjoyment of life?*

—John Powell

How often do we think, *I'd be happy if . . .* or *I'll be
happy when . . . ?* How often have we felt calm, content,
and self-satisfied, only to plunge into fear, anger, or
despair when something happened, or didn't happen,
in our lives? Or even when we just heard about something happening to someone else? How many conditions in our outer lives do we believe are necessary for
happiness within?

Sometimes we convince ourselves that we'll be happy
when we lose some weight, get a job or promotion,
find a loving relationship, get married, have a baby, or
achieve some other outer goal. But when the goal is
accomplished, there are always others to take its place.
Happiness always seems to be just beyond our reach.

We've all seen bumper stickers and posters declaring
Murphy's Law: "Anything that can go wrong, will." And
yet, when something does go wrong, we're often surprised. We feel confused, caught off guard, thrown off
balance, and even angry. Our serenity and happiness
may fly right out the window. Whatever we felt we
needed to be all right is gone, and now where are we?

The reality is that cars sometimes break down, sales-people are sometimes rude, reservations get mixed up, and dates are broken. Our heroes may suddenly prove to be weak or corrupt. The addicts in our lives may choose not to recover. People we love may die or move away. We may lose our jobs, relationships, health, or money. All of our bodies will age. Things happen and things change—that's the nature of life.

Is it possible to live in this world, with all its confusion, pain, and injustice, and not be affected by it all? Of course not. The questions are, *how* are we affected, and *how much?* Does a chance remark from a co-worker send us into a depression? Do news stories about accidents, catastrophes, or crimes destroy our faith in elevators, airplanes, or people? Does a salesclerk's mistake make us so angry that we refuse to shop in the same place ever again? Does a five minute phone conversation with a relative fill us with guilt or worry for hours, or even days?

How much of our happiness and serenity are we willing to turn over to the outer circumstances of life? If we *know* things can and will go wrong, why do we still seek perfection? Why do we put off being happy, acting as if someday everything will begin going our way? Why do we allow everything that happens outside us to create a wild roller coaster of thoughts, feelings, and attitudes inside us?

Clearly, *knowing* the nature of things in the outer world is not the same as *accepting* it. For most of us, Murphy's Law is a bitter complaint. But does it have to be? What if we peacefully accepted the reality that often, things just will not go our way? What if we truly believed, deep in our hearts, that we'd be all right no matter what happened in our outer lives or in the world?

As long as we make outer conditions responsible for our inner states of mind, we'll live on a roller coaster of intense emotions. As long as we can only be happy when our team wins, we'll be unhappy a lot of the time. As long as we keep setting goals for future happiness, serenity, and contentment, we'll never reach that elusive gold at the end of the rainbow.

The world is not set up to go your way or my way or anyone else's way. Murphy's Law, like most platitudes, contains a great deal of truth. But rather than an expression of resentment and self-pity, it can be a guiding light to remind us that we *can* live with the realities of this world. We can face them with humor, flexibility, and serenity. We really can be okay, no matter what happens.

Equanimity

How do we achieve this state of self-control and inner peace? By discovering the endless well of acceptance and tranquility which lives deep within each of us. There is a place inside every one of us where only love and peace and total equanimity reign. *Equanimity* is a word we don't hear much these days. It means an evenness of temper, a calmness and peacefulness of mind, body, and heart.

Almost a hundred years ago, James Allen wrote, in a little book called *As A Man Thinketh,* "Who does not love a tranquil heart, a sweet-tempered, balanced life? It does not matter whether it rains or shines, or what changes come to those possessing these sweet blessings, for they are always sweet, serene, and calm." This is *equanimity,* and that's what this book is all about.

We can begin our journey toward this place of inner peace and balance by reminding ourselves often of the Serenity Prayer, and contemplating its true meaning.

God grant me the serenity
To accept the things I cannot change,
The courage to change the things I can,
And the wisdom to know the difference.

Accepting what we can't change means fully enjoying a ball game, regardless of who wins. It means knowing that the world will not end if we change jobs, take a later flight, or can't afford that new car. It means knowing that the world and all its people are not perfect—and *that's okay.* True acceptance means more than grudging tolerance; it means our inner peace and happiness aren't threatened by any outside event or situation.

But is there still a little voice telling us that this is somehow irresponsible? In his book, *Notes on How to Live in the World . . . and Still Be Happy,* Hugh Prather writes, "There is entrenched guilt over lightheartedness and great fear that when we take time to be happy we are not guarding our own interests, and certainly not doing all we can for the world."

Let's ask ourselves what all our worrying, complaining, fearfulness, and anger are really doing for ourselves, anyone else, or the world. Constant vigilance over all the world and other people's problems doesn't alleviate them in any way. Our belief that we are somehow safer from those dangers that we think a lot about are usually delusions. Many of our fears and worries are about things that will never touch our lives. But we may still feel guilty for wanting, expecting, or pursuing real happiness and contentment in life.

Can we use inner peace as an excuse for unpaid bills, unfulfilled promises, or carelessly destructive behavior? Of course not. In the Serenity Prayer, we ask for the courage to change the things we *can,* and this is where our personal responsibilities lie. The only things we can change are ourselves. We are completely responsible for our own thoughts, actions, and attitudes. We fulfill our responsibilities and contribute positively to the world around us by doing our very best in these areas. And our best gets better and better with time, practice, and not wasting time and energy on things we can never control.

Taking responsibility for our happiness doesn't mean we'll never again face difficulties. Sometimes, things we don't expect will happen, and things we do expect won't happen. We won't always get what we think we want, and what we do get won't always turn out to be so great. We'll still feel hurt, sad, disappointed, and angry from time to time. But these feelings don't have to cut so deeply or last so long that they ruin our day, week, or life.

Developing our inner strength, serenity, and spiritual growth will enable us, more and more, to peacefully accept whatever happens outside ourselves. The ups and downs of life will become more like gently rolling hills instead of terrifying peaks and gut-wrenching valleys.

When we learn to truly know ourselves, love ourselves, and center our personal energy in our highest spiritual selves, we'll *know*— deeply and certainly—that we'll be okay no matter what happens to or around us. We'll know that even feeling bad for a while is sometimes all right. We'll let go of the past and trust that the future will bring nothing we can't deal with, learn from, and grow through. The only condition required for finding true peace and happiness is that we look for it in the only place it can be found—deep within ourselves.

In this book, we'll look at our beliefs about happiness, spirituality, work, money, other people, our bodies, and our surroundings. We'll see how we've allowed the outer circumstances of our lives to determine our inner states of mind. We'll also discover new ways of looking at old situations, and positive ways to change the things we can. We'll find new truth and joy in some old platitudes, and learn to apply them in our lives.

We'll discover a new kind of happiness that doesn't depend on any outer condition. We'll start growing toward that peaceful, happy state of *equanimity*. We won't create lives free of hills and valleys, but we just might start learning to enjoy the ride.

CHAPTER TWO

Happiness

How to gain, how to keep, how to recover happiness, is in fact for most people at all times the secret motive for all they do and all they are willing to endure.

—William James

Everyone has a personal happiness history. Throughout our lives, we've defined and experienced happiness in many ways. If we examine these histories, we can learn about our growth and development toward a more mature experience of happiness.

Kara's Happiness History

"For most of my life I was a pretty unhappy person," Kara tells us. "The alcoholism in my family filled my childhood with fear, mistrust, anger, and confusion. I fantasized that when I grew up everything would be different, and I would live happily ever after.

"In my teens," Kara continues, "I had already learned to shut down my feelings and avoid pain by convincing myself that I didn't care about anyone or anything. I planned to devote my life to a career and keep people at a distance. On the surface, I believed that life was misery and nothing really mattered very much. Secretly, I still expected to live happily ever after—someday."

Kara spent her twenties caretaking, approval seeking, and people pleasing. "I felt that my underlying unhappiness was somehow my fault," she says, "that there was something wrong with me for feeling unhappy while the outer conditions of my life seemed relatively good."

The year she turned thirty, something changed inside Kara. "I started feeling that if I was ever going to 'live happily ever after' it was going to be now or never. I examined everything in my life, and decided to keep what was good and get rid of everything I thought was making me unhappy. I quit a job I hated and took a lower-paying one I loved. I went back to college on loans, scholarships, and determination. I made several other changes in my outer life, but more importantly, I started looking at life as possibilities and opportunities, rather than obligations and dangerous traps.

"The only thing that really changed that year was in my mind," Kara says. "All the changes in my outer life had been available to me all along, but I simply couldn't see them until I gave myself permission to see them.

"That was only the first step on my journey toward inner peace and true happiness. I've since learned that it wasn't the job, school, or anything else outside myself that made me happy. *It was my decision to start being happy.* It was my choice to open up to learning where happiness could be found. It was letting go of some old beliefs, behaviors, and relationships, and accepting some new ones into my life. It was the discovery that *the answer was in me all along.*"

Everyone Wants to Be Happy

We think about it, talk about it, and sing songs about it. We wish, plan, hope, pray, and long for it. Even our biggest mistakes and most self-defeating behaviors come from a desire to somehow make ourselves happy.

Everyone recognizes happiness as a necessary, or at least desirable, ingredient in life. But what exactly *is* happiness? Does everyone define and experience it in the same way? Why do some people seem happier than others, regardless of their circumstances? What makes a person happy?

Old Definitions

Most of us probably define happiness as getting something we want, or getting relief from something we don't want. Therefore, we define happiness differently, depending on what we happen to want at any given time. We give responsibility for our happiness to some outer condition in our life.

We may believe that happiness requires a certain kind of freedom, such as a vacation from school or work. We may feel that physical pleasure and comfort are necessary for our happiness. Some of us may surround ourselves with luxurious amenities or spend our time seeking the highs of food, sex, drugs, or whatever else we think will make us feel good.

We may believe that excitement is the essential ingredient in happiness, and therefore create drama or even danger in our lives. We may keep moving from place to place, ending and beginning relationships, changing our job, dress, or lifestyle as frequently as possible.

We may feel that happiness comes from the approval and acceptance of others, and so we strive to succeed in whatever ways we feel will impress those around us. Or we may spend our time and energy trying to make others happy, with the underlying expectation that they, in turn, will make us happy.

Old Sources

These beliefs came from our childhood homes, families, schools, churches, and society at large. The images we receive from television and other mass media influence our beliefs and attitudes enormously. But our families of origin still have the biggest impact on our belief system.

Even if our parents' way of seeking happiness clearly failed, we did not fail to take in their instruction—either verbal or by example—about how to live and seek happiness. We may tend to believe on some level that our parents simply failed at their task, rather than examining the task itself. And so we believe that we will succeed where they failed, and proceed to behave much as they did.

Old Effects

Whatever our beliefs about happiness, we are doomed to failure in finding it as long as we expect it to be triggered by outer circumstances, which are always changing. We will spend our lives pursuing temporary "fixes" of happiness. Our inner longing for true happiness will go forever unsatisfied.

If we define happiness as a state of perfection, with everything going exactly as we'd like, we'll never be happy. If we feel dependent on another person for our happiness, we resign ourselves to misery and pain whenever he or she doesn't do what we want or expect. If we define happiness as pleasure, excitement, or adventure, our happiness will at best be transient and erratic. It could also lead to disease, danger, or tragedy.

Happiness Is a Choice

Happiness is a feeling inside us that everything is all right. It is the absence of fear, confusion, and conflict. It is a place of rest, contentment, and joy. It is peace of mind. The most important thing to learn about happiness, I believe, is that it is a *choice*. We always have it available to us; it's within each of us.

What we need to remember is that there's always another way of looking at anything. When we are unhappy—that is, when we are out of touch with our basic, natural peace and contentment—it is because we have gotten our minds stuck in an unhappy point of view. We cling stubbornly to this viewpoint, losing sight of our alternatives. And even in difficult circumstances, there are always alternatives.

Happiness and Guilt

If happiness is a constant choice, why would anyone choose otherwise? This may be because we either don't know we have the choice, or we feel we don't deserve it. We choose guilt, fear, or worry about things we can't control, instead of choosing happiness.

In her book, *Love & Guilt & the Meaning of Life, Etc.*, Judith Viorst writes, "Show me a happy person and I'll show you a very worried human being, a human being who is always asking, What did I do to deserve such happiness? And, What and how much am I going to have to pay for it?"

There may also be a tendency toward arrogance in our unhappiness. We may view people who seem happy as frivolous, selfish, or not very bright. In the late 1980s, when Bobby McFerrin sang "Don't Worry, Be Happy," some people took it as a call to hedonistic irresponsibility. Their guilt was triggered, and they

11

equated the song with Timothy Leary's "tune in, turn on, and drop out" ethic of the 1960s. Only if we value worry, if we believe we can control everything, and if we view happiness as bad, can a simple, positive phrase like "don't worry, be happy" seem so ominous.

Happiness could only have gotten such a bad reputation as long as we defined it as irresponsible pleasure seeking. Since we all want happiness, this definition keeps us in constant conflict over the desire for happiness and the desire to be good, responsible people. Our confusion comes from many sources. Religion and our social conscience are two powerful sources for guilt over happiness.

Happiness and Religion

Religion has sometimes, throughout the ages, attempted to encourage good, loving behavior by condemning our desire for happiness. We may have been taught, directly or indirectly, that misery, suffering, and self-sacrifice somehow make us good. It's important to remember that our religious affiliations are not the same as our relationship with God. Our priests, ministers, and rabbis are only human. They may inadvertently or mistakenly lead us to fear happiness.

However, we can look at religion in another way without throwing it out altogether. In the classic story, *Pollyanna,* the heroine reminds a conflicted minister that the Bible contains over 800 directives for us to be happy. Pollyanna declares, "If God took the trouble to tell us *800 times* to be glad and rejoice, He must have wanted us to do it!" The clarity and simplicity of this child's view cut right through our religious rationalizations and excuses for guilt over happiness.

Ninety-year-old Marie remembers the advice her father gave her when she was growing up in a small village in Italy. "He always made me go to church, no matter how much I complained about the sermons of the old priest in our village," she says. "But my father used to say, 'You don't have to listen to the priest if you don't want to. Just don't pay any attention to him. But go and say your prayers in God's house.'" Marie credits her strong lifelong faith in God to her father's advice. He taught her what Twelve Step programs tell us today—*take what you can use, and leave the rest.* This is as true for religion as it is for Twelve Step programs. Because she didn't "throw out the baby with the bathwater," Marie's faith grew and flourished over the years and became the bedrock of her happiness.

The Politics of Happiness

Another source of conflict over happiness comes from our social and political life. How can we be happy when there is so much war, hunger, homelessness, poverty, disease, injustice, ignorance, cruelty, and suffering in the world? How can we be aware, concerned, and instrumental in making positive change, and be *happy* at the same time?

It's easy to feel discouraged or depressed over all the problems in the world. But discouragement and depression have never caused any positive change. Worry, anger, fear, and sadness may make us feel righteous, aware, concerned, and informed, but they contribute nothing to the alleviation or elimination of the problems. Coupling any action with a negative viewpoint is self-defeating and counterproductive. But positive action that comes from a positive attitude can create powerful change. Choosing our own true inner happiness enables us to spread that positive energy out into the world.

I believe the happiest people on the face of the earth are those who are truly making a positive contribution to humanity. Did Mother Teresa worry that her work with the poor was only a tiny drop in the enormous sea of human suffering? Choosing such a negative outlook would surely have made it impossible for her to get up every morning and do the wonderful work she did. Without a deep, underlying sense of faith, hope, and peace—which are primary elements of true happiness—how could she have brought so much love to others? Our unhappiness doesn't help anyone or make the world a better place.

A New Concept of Happiness

Once we overcome the obstacles of believing that a deep, constant, underlying happiness is either impossible or immoral, we can move on to discovering what it is and how we can find and maintain it.

When we turn away from our belief in happiness as fleeting moments of relief between crises and pain, we can begin seeing it as our basic well-being. We can think of well-being as far more than the absence of disease or pain. It is a basic, constant faith that all is, or will be, well. Even when things happen that seem difficult or painful, well-being is the knowledge that we can survive, take care of ourselves, learn, grow, and recover our equilibrium. It is *balance,* so that even high winds, torrential rains, and crashing waves can't throw us overboard.

Real, true, lasting happiness isn't found in adventure, excitement, or physical comfort or pleasure. It is not obtained through pleasing other people or driving ourselves toward some imaginary state of perfection. It is only found in quiet contentment, faith, hope, and tranquility.

Contentment

Learning to be content is a huge step toward true happiness. It means accepting things as they are, not trying to control them, and seeing all the good there is to see everywhere. The Talmud, the Jewish book of rabbinic teachings, tells us that a rich man is one who is content with what he has. The Serenity Prayer reminds us that acceptance of the things we can't control is the key to living peacefully and happily.

Contentment doesn't mean complacency, fatalism, or denial. As Paul Pearsall writes in his book, *Super Joy,* "There is a real difference between denying real problems and the avoidance of agonizing over those things we cannot change." Contentment means being fully wherever we are right now, and knowing that this is where we need to be. We can still hope and plan and work toward a better future, but all the while concentrating on the good that is at hand.

Faith

Happiness comes from our way of looking at the world, our basic beliefs and attitudes toward life. Faith is a fundamental part of our worldview. I believe there is no such thing as a faithless person. The question is only *where* we place our faith.

Some of us have faith in our careers, political beliefs, or scientific knowledge. Others of us may place our faith in our own intellectual abilities, our bodies, or our personalities. Some of us turn to food, sex, drugs, money, or alcohol as the object of our faith. Many of us put our faith in other people—our families, friends, lovers, or political or religious leaders.

But sometimes our true faith is hidden beneath one of these labels. For example, two people may both say they have faith in God. One of them may see God as a totally loving, accepting, understanding, and forgiving spirit to whom she will return in blissful communion whenever God chooses to end her life on earth. The other may see God as a judgmental, angry, punishing, unforgiving ogre who will cast her into excruciating and eternal pain if she displeases him. These two people have clearly placed their faith in two very different gods—one, love; the other, fear.

Developing our own concept of a positive, loving, helpful Higher Power is important to discovering the deep, inner happiness we seek. When we shift our faith from people and circumstances outside ourselves to our own spirituality and connection to our Higher Power, we find all the elements of happiness within us.

There can be an infinite number of images of a Higher Power, but what is important is that we see our Higher Power as loving, forgiving, understanding, peaceful, gentle, and kind. Our Higher Power is the force that can heal us and help us grow. It is the wisdom we need to guide us through our lives.

Hope

Leo Buscaglia writes in *Bus 9 to Paradise,* "The world is full of possibilities, and as long as there are possibilities, there is hope." We can only lose hope when we refuse to see the possibilities. For example, losing a job is not the end of the world. We can look for another similar one, try a new line of work, go back to school, or move to another place where jobs are more plentiful.

We can try starting our own business, selling handmade goods, or offering needed services. Our options are almost unlimited. Hope opens our minds to the confidence that we can do something other than what we may have planned on, that there are always other possibilities.

We choose hopelessness in many ways. We decide it's the end of the world if we don't get a specific thing we want. We refuse to try things before we really know whether or not they'll work. We expect the future to repeat the past, assuming things can't ever be different. The greatest assertion of hope I have read was written by George Bernard Shaw and made famous in a speech by Robert Kennedy: "Some see things as they are and ask 'Why?'; I dream things that never were, and ask, 'Why not?'"

Hope is that part of us that never gives up, that *knows* we will be all right with complete certainty and trust. It's the part of us that says, *I may be going through a dark tunnel right now, but I know there is a light at the end, even if I can't see it yet.*

Hope is essential for human beings. It's a wonderful gift we all have at our disposal, all the time. It's what keeps us alive. When we believe in our future, in the future of others and of the world, we can endure the present with courage and joy. Even if we can only see our way clear to hoping for one good day, *today,* that's enough. Tomorrow we can hope again for another good day. The world is indeed full of possibilities.

Tranquility

Words like *tranquility, equanimity,* and *serenity* may be beautiful, but what do they really mean? They mean balance, peace, and calmness. They mean the absence of conflict, fear, and worry. They mean reaching into that quiet place within each of us, where all the worries, frustrations, and aggravations of life have no meaning.

In a wonderful little book called, *The Majesty of Calmness,* William George Jordan wrote, "Calmness comes from within. It is the peace and restfulness of the depths of our nature. The fury of storm and of wind agitate only the surface of the sea . . . below that is the calm, unruffled deep. To be ready for the great crises of life we must learn serenity in our daily living. Calmness is the crown of self-control." When we control ourselves by not reacting quickly out of anger, fear, or despair, we give our natural inner peace a chance to take over.

Redefining Happiness

Author Hugh Prather writes, "Happiness is gentleness, peace, concentration, simplicity, forgiveness, humor, fearlessness, trust, and now." This wonderful explanation describes not only what happiness looks and feels like, but also where and how to get it. Notice that none of the elements listed are conditions outside ourselves. They are attitudes, points of view, *choices* we can all make.

We feel gentleness by being gentle; peace of mind by behaving peacefully; concentration by using our minds to focus on inner well-being and happiness. We find simplicity in our lives by simplifying our thoughts, attitudes, beliefs, and lifestyles. We feel the blessing of forgiveness by forgiving. We become light-hearted by choosing the perception of humor. We become fearless by letting go of our harbored fears and turning them over to our Higher Power. We begin to know trust by allowing our Higher Power to work in our lives. And the time to do all of this is *now*.

If we remember to be gentle, peaceful, focused on joy and contentment, clear and uncomplicated in our thoughts and desires, forgiving toward ourselves and others, open to humor, fearless, trusting in our Higher Power, and always fully present in the now, we will indeed be happy. And if we are happy, all these things will follow.

Choosing Happiness

Throughout this book, we will examine our beliefs in a *pragmatic* way. In other words, we will ask ourselves what *effects* our beliefs have on us, others, and the world. If our beliefs are not having positive effects on our outlook and experience of life, we can change them. We can remember Hugh Prather's definition of happiness, and develop a new belief system.

When we place our faith in a positive, loving force or God, we can trust the general goodness of life, regardless of day-to-day upsets. When we concentrate on peace rather than conflict, gentleness rather than aggression, joy rather than pain, and love rather than fear, we can discover the peace, gentleness, joy, and love that were there all along. We can choose happiness.

Let's now define happiness as our highest well-being. Let's focus on this new concept of happiness as we face life's daily challenges. *Be happy first.* Let your natural inner happiness guide your choices. Then take care of your daily business and cope with whatever happens. Pursue whatever outer circumstances you want, but remember that they, in themselves, will not create your happiness, and that if they aren't satisfied, *you will still be all right.* Let true happiness come out from deep within you and take its rightful place at the center of your life.

Exercises

Exercise One

Write Your Own Happiness History. Examine your beliefs and attitudes toward your own well-being and happiness. See how your beliefs and attitudes have changed over the years. How would you like to change them now to help you find your highest well-being and happiness?

Exercise Two

Play the "Glad Game." This was Pollyanna's game of finding something to be glad about in everything. Find something positive, however small, in every event, relationship, situation, and person in your life. Play this game every day, several times a day, until it becomes second nature to you.

Exercise Three

Feel Your Happiness. Define true happiness clearly for yourself. Not what you think you need to have it, but what it *feels* like to you. Close your eyes and find the place deep inside you where this feeling lives. Go to that place and feel happiness—love, peace, gentleness, joy, trust, hope, and fearlessness—filling you up inside. Try to recall this feeling in various places and situations. Discover that you can feel this peaceful contentment whenever and wherever you choose.

CHAPTER THREE

Our Identity

Every decision that you make stems from what you think you are, and represents the value that you put upon yourself.

—A Course in Miracles

Our personal identity and self-image affect all that we think, feel, and do. What we believe of ourselves is fundamental to our perspective on everything. If we see ourselves as merely bodies and conscious minds, we are likely to remain unhappily searching for perfection in these areas. If we see ourselves as incapable of love, peace, joy, cooperation, and forgiveness, we won't be able to see the opportunities for them in our lives.

Human beings have struggled with the question of identity since the beginning of time. We have turned to philosophy, religion, and science for the answers, and countless theories, ideas, and possibilities have evolved. But we often become disillusioned and even angry when these answers prove to be imperfect or incomplete. The truth is, at this point in history, we just don't know the meaning of life with absolute certainty.

We all want to find a clear, simple understanding of ourselves and our world. But just as no one can control everything, no one can know everything. Once we accept it, we can live with this limitation quite fully and happily. We don't have to have all the answers, and even more, we *can't have all the answers*. This acceptance frees us to be more open to hearing the truths already whispering in our hearts. Acknowledging our confusion can be the first step toward letting go of our old, self-defeating beliefs and behaviors.

When we give up our desire for indisputable evidence of absolute truths, we can begin to accept some comforting, helpful, guiding ideas. Once we accept that there may always be some unanswered questions, we can choose our beliefs about being human based on whether they enhance our lives and the contributions we make to others. We can choose to view life and ourselves in ways that help us live better, healthier, happier lives.

To each of us, "truth" is made up of our own perceptions. Whether or not we realize it, we are always choosing our perceptions, beliefs, attitudes, and behaviors. When we begin choosing consciously, we can learn to avoid those that cause our unhappiness and self-defeating actions. We can pragmatically choose those perceptions that help us, instead of those that hurt us.

Man or Butterfly?

There is an ancient Chinese legend about a man who dreamt he was a butterfly. It was the loveliest dream imaginable. He felt himself floating about through the air, light and free. He felt completely, blissfully happy. Everything in this dream was beautiful, peaceful, and joyous. According to the legend, when the man awoke from this dream, he was never again certain whether he was really a man who had dreamt he was a butterfly, or a butterfly who now dreamt he was a man.

This story illustrates the split we feel as human beings. We are uncertain of our identity—are we body, mind, emotions, or spirit? Are we naturally loving, peaceful, happy, angry, afraid, aggressive, or cooperative? All of these things, and more, seem to be part of being human, but some get more attention than others—they're noisier. It's hard to ignore a feeling of rage within us, and easy to miss the quiet voice of peacefulness, gentleness, and love. But that doesn't mean the loving part isn't there.

To simplify this whole confusing picture, let's stick with the idea of the man/butterfly. Let's call all of those noisy feelings, thoughts, beliefs, and actions our *ego*. This is the "man" part of us—fearful, defensive, angry, territorial, and worried. This part of us keenly feels the needs and desires of survival and pleasure, and in fact, feels nothing else. In his book, *Goodbye to Guilt,* Jerry Jampolsky defines our ego as, "our body/personality or lower self."

But also within each of us lives a higher self, a *butterfly:* a purely loving, peaceful, joyous spirit untouched by anything in the outer world. This part of us is quiet, gentle, peaceful, forgiving, accepting, and fearless. From Plato to Spinoza to Thornton Wilder, humans have always expressed a feeling that we are somehow eternal. This butterfly, or *spirit,* is the eternal part of us, the part that is free of the cares and concerns of the world and is connected to our Higher Power and to the spirits of all other people.

Ego or Spirit?

In the first chapter, I said that there is always another way of looking at anything, and that we choose unhappiness by getting stuck in one point of view. While situations often seem complex, there are really only two ways of looking at anything—from the viewpoint of our ego or the viewpoint of our spirit.

Author Hugh Prather writes about our "happy self" and our "unhappy self." M. Scott Peck writes, "We all have a sick self and a healthy self." I use the words "ego" and "spirit" for these same two parts of us. One part is sick, unhappy, self-destructive, and based on a self-image that we are a separate mind, body, and personality. The other is healthy, happy, constructive, and based on a self-knowledge that we are part of one harmonious whole with all others and God.

Whenever something seems to be making us unhappy, we can remember to ask ourselves which point of view we are choosing. Our ego's viewpoint is easy to spot if we look for fear, hopelessness, anger, or a strong desire to be right or prove someone else wrong. On the other hand, our spirit's point of view is always calm, loving, accepting, gentle, peaceful, and fearless.

In every case, we choose between the viewpoint of either our ego (man) or our spirit (butterfly). There is no other point of view. But this split within us can be bridged by allowing the loving, peaceful part of us to guide and help the fearful, self-defeating part. Our spirit can lead our ego to behave sanely, lovingly, and happily. For this, we need to use our mind as a liaison between our ego and our spirit.

Using Our Minds

John Milton wrote, "The mind is its own place, and in itself can make a heaven of hell, a hell of heaven." Our mind chooses which viewpoint to see—our ego's or our spirit's. It can live in a self-imposed hell of fearful, angry thoughts, or a heaven of loving, peaceful thoughts. But we can choose how to use our mind.

For example, if someone says something unkind to us, our ego will probably immediately perceive this as an attack against which it must defend itself. It will fill us with anger, hostility, and fear. It may prompt us to attack the other person verbally or in some other way. But if we understand our ego and its frightened, defensive viewpoint, we can turn to our other way of seeing—the way of our spirit. Our mind can see our spirit's loving, forgiving, understanding perspective, and help our ego to calm down and temper its response.

Since we are both ego and spirit, we can't always behave in a perfectly loving way. But we can take control of our actions before our ego gets carried away and causes harm. If we've already caused harm, we can still find our spirit's perspective after we've calmed down, and then make appropriate amends.

As we become more accustomed to seeing ourselves as responding either from our ego or our spirit, we can learn to recognize our ego's feelings and reactions more quickly, and let our spirit take over sooner. Our unhappy, self-defeating feelings and behaviors can become less intense and long-lasting.

Simplifying our view of our reactions, beliefs, feelings, and behaviors by identifying them as either belonging to our ego or spirit can help us accept ourselves and improve our lives. We don't have to be angry or impatient with ourselves. That would only be our ego fighting against itself. Instead, we can accept that we have these two parts or viewpoints within us, and learn to work with them to produce the best results.

Our Ego

In his play, *Our Town,* Thornton Wilder wrote, "Whenever you come near the human race, there's layers and layers of nonsense." Our ego is the part of us that creates these layers and layers of nonsense. Egos are not inherently *bad,* they simply have certain capabilities, limitations, and a specific viewpoint. It is not our goal to eradicate our ego, even if that were possible. But rather, we can learn to understand it, accept it, and use it for our highest well-being.

Our ego can be thought of as a level of consciousness that includes much of what we think of as ourselves, including our bodies and personalities. It is convinced that it *is* us, complete in itself. It misinterprets everything and creates our self-defeating behaviors and beliefs. It convinces us that it can make us safe and happy, but it never does.

Our ego is the part of us that always needs to be right, to have the last word. It values conflict and always feels threatened. Its only modes of communication are attack and defend. But it often disguises these with elaborate rationalizations and justifications. It denies, lies, tricks, confuses, hurts, blames, hates, and fears. And all the while, it is certain that it is acting only in our best interests.

Games Egos Play

The first step in learning to think and act from the viewpoint of our spirit is to recognize our ego's characteristic traits. We have already talked about fearfulness, anger, defensiveness, and hopelessness. But our ego also has many deceptive ways of persuading us to follow its misguidance. When we learn to recognize these traps, we can begin avoiding them.

Denial

One of our ego's favorite games is denial. It persuades us to remain ignorant of real dangers and mistakes because to face them would mean re-evaluating our choices from another viewpoint. Our ego tends to see every other viewpoint as its enemy—even our loving, peaceful spirit's. Our ego thinks reality will destroy it. If we refuse to see the realities around us, we can believe anything our ego wants us to.

Rationalization

Human beings can make just about anything seem to make sense if we try hard enough. We can justify almost any action with "good" motives. This is our ego's way of keeping us from seeing the mistake in its basic point of view. Rationalization uses our mind's reasoning to believe seemingly sensible excuses and "reasons" for self-defeating, destructive, or unhappy beliefs and behaviors.

Blame

Our ego always finds someone or some outer circumstance to blame for our unhappiness and mistakes. It always sees someone as wrong and someone as right—and it always needs to be right. We avoid accepting our powerlessness over others and our responsibility for ourselves by viewing all of our setbacks and problems as caused by terrible forces working against us. We stay bogged down in anger and self-pity instead of letting go of the past, other people, and uncontrollable circumstances.

Competition

Since our ego sees all others as enemies, it can never accept or enjoy the successes of others. It only feels good about itself if it is somehow better than someone else. And then the feeling is false and fleeting—there is *always* someone better than us in some way. The ego never accepts this, and so it continues to make us feel bad about not being the best at everything all the time.

Our ego's strong belief in deprivation says, "If you're succeeding or gaining in some way, you're taking something away from *me.*" Thus, it must always compete for everything good, since it can't understand sharing or believe that there is enough good to go around.

Complication

Simple, clear, even obvious answers do not appeal to our ego. The ego can be thought of as a dog perpetually chasing its tail: it can keep us going on and on in an endless struggle, rather than face a simple truth. Instead, it convinces us that everything is complex and difficult, rather than open to simple solutions and a loving, accepting, forgiving, positive viewpoint.

Our ego says, *Even if peace, love, and joy were possible, they'd be boring!* To our ego, complication and stress feel more alive than simplicity and peacefulness. And thus it avoids the joy of love, peace, and cooperation.

Projection

Projection is when we refuse to see our own thoughts, beliefs, attitudes, mistakes, or behaviors, but we see them in others. This allows us to avoid responsibility for ourselves and to not see our feelings and reactions from another perspective. It's a blaming, defensive standpoint from which we don't have to face the realities of our misperceptions and mistakes. Jerry Jampolsky calls projection, "a mechanism that says, 'the enemy is outside ourselves.'" In fact, the enemy—what's hurting us—is the ego within ourselves.

Attachment

Attachment is the basic attitude that we must have certain conditions in order to be happy. Our ego is certain that happiness is found outside ourselves. The main feature of this aspect of our ego is that it is *never satisfied*. Whatever the ego attaches itself to is never enough. There is always something better tomorrow, and the next day, and again the next. The ego's goals are many, always changing, and often conflicting.

Transference

Transference is the term used in psychotherapy for responding to present relationships and situations as if they were those of the past. Our ego convinces us that the past accurately predicts the future, so we neglect to be fully present and open to the real possibilities here and now. We see the present through a fog of old misunderstandings and judgments. We repeat the same mistakes over and over, without realizing we are doing it ourselves. We remain focused on the transgressions of the past, unable to see our present opportunities and responsibilities. Our true identity as spiritual beings can only be found in the present, so our ego avoids facing this by focusing on the past.

Body Equals Self

Our ego doesn't want to acknowledge that we are anything but *it*. It feels threatened and won't accept that it can live peacefully and happily in cooperation with our spirit. When we begin awakening to our spirituality, it will often become fearful and try to distract us from this revelation. It may use pain, illness, hunger, or sex to convince us that we are nothing more than our bodies. It may find ways to remind us of our physical separateness from others, keeping us from the realization that we are all connected in our spirituality and our Higher Power.

Fear

Fear is our ego's trademark and primary characteristic. It is afraid of everything, perceiving threats everywhere. It keeps us enmeshed in worry about the future. This fear can immobilize us, impede our growth, and harm every area of our lives. It can hold us back from love, peace, joy, and serenity. It can keep us apart from other people, and our own best selves. It is our ego's mistaken belief that it's protecting us, taking care of us, helping us. But it's the main obstacle standing between us and our true success and happiness in life.

* * * * *

Our ego will never change of itself. It's like a child who is incapable of growing up. This is why we so often react and behave in self-defeating ways even long after we feel we know better. But our ego does not have to rule us. We can learn to recognize its confusion, its mistakes, its fear, and its pain. We can learn to choose love over fear, and joy over pain.

Our Spirit

Our spirit is our ego's direct opposite in many ways. It's incapable of feeling anger, pain, worry, fear, or sorrow. It never feels threatened in any way, because it is absolutely certain of its invulnerability. It knows itself to be eternal, at one with all other spirits, and connected to a Higher Power.

Our spirit is only capable of unlimited love and joy. It has no interest in who is right or wrong. It has no use for conflict. It values peace, love, and sharing above all else. It recognizes the abundance of the universe as infinite and available to all of us, always. It only offers unconditional love, acceptance, and forgiveness. It is purely joyful, generous, content, and gentle, and always knows our true best interests.

Others' Spirits

Recognizing our own spirituality can transform our self-image, behavior, and lives. Likewise, recognizing the spirit in others can transform our outlook and all of our relationships. But it's sometimes difficult to see the good, spiritual part of another person, especially when he or she has done harmful things or expresses a callous, self-centered attitude.

We can begin by recognizing that everyone has an ego that is always afraid and acting out self-defeating beliefs. We can think, with understanding, *Look at what their* ego *did,* instead of thinking, with condemnation, *Look at what* they *did.* If we take a moment to let our initial ego-reaction pass, and to overlook the ego-reactions of others, we can move beyond them to more peaceful, happy relations with other people. This can help us stop defining people as their egos, and we can begin overlooking and forgiving their faults and mis-

31

takes. Then, instead of searching for what we can judge as *good* in them (which can sometimes be very hard to find), we can simply *know* that they also have within them a perfect, loving spirit—even if we can't see it beneath all those layers and layers of ego-nonsense.

Spiritual Growth

I don't believe our spirits need to grow or evolve at all. I believe they are already perfect. What spiritual growth or evolution means to me is that we human beings need to grow in our awareness of this spiritual aspect of ourselves and get to know it. We need to learn to see its viewpoint and hear its guidance. Then we can learn to extend its qualities out into our lives and the world. This way our spirit grows in the sense of expanding, touching the spirits in others, and growing together with them.

Every day, situation, and relationship contains opportunities to open up to our spirit's viewpoint and guidance. Everywhere are chances for us to extend the highest, best, spiritual part of ourselves out into the world. No matter who we are, or what our particular circumstances might be, we can all discover the power and peace of our spirituality.

We have to take the time needed for spiritual growth, and not allow ourselves to become impatient. There is no end to the wondrous discoveries we can make on this journey. But we have to allow them to unfold in their own time. It may take many months, or even years, for us to see that we have turned a corner in our spiritual evolution. As the meditation book, *God Calling,* reminds us, "When climbing a steep hill, a man is often more conscious of the weakness of his stumbling feet than of the view, the grandeur, or even of his upward progress."

Faith, hope, and persistence will keep us growing spiritually.

Our Inner Truth

Because our egos are so noisy and demanding, they often obscure our awareness of our spirituality. But since we can never experience true happiness through our ego, we feel a nagging sense of dissatisfaction until we turn to our spirit. When we are in conflict within ourselves, that conflict is reflected in our outer lives. It's a kind of self-betrayal to place our center of personal energy outside our true selves, as we do when we define ourselves as our egos. It makes us sick, tired, and unhappy to go against our own inner truth.

We must each experience our spirituality for ourselves. Reading, thinking, talking, or writing about it doesn't give us the *experience* of it. These things may help us move in the direction needed to open ourselves up to our own spirituality, but eventually, we must turn inward.

Deep inside, we all know that we are spiritual beings. As long as we ignore this part of ourselves, we may feel a kind of gnawing ache, like a vague memory, a yearning for something we can't quite name. We may feel a sort of homesickness for our spirits whenever we recognize great beauty or experience moments of unconditional love. We may experience brief flashes of inspiration or perfect peace, when we *know* we are something more than our egos.

There is a sense of familiarity, of *coming home,* in discovering—or rather, *re*discovering— our spirituality. It's like hearing an old song, suddenly remembering where you were when you first heard it and who you were with, and recalling the feelings you had then.

Think of an old love song that reminds you of a special person you once knew. How much more powerful, more beautiful, more moving is the recognition of our spirituality than even this fond memory!

Only when we rediscover our spirit and begin letting it grow into our conscious awareness can we experience the peace of harmony and balance between our bodies, minds, and spirits. For some of us, this begins with a transformational experience—a spiritual awakening.

Spiritual Awakening

In *The Varieties of Religious Experience,* William James identified the following characteristics of a spiritual experience:

- It defies description; it must be experienced first-hand to be understood.

- It brings a sense of certainty, of knowledge or profound insight into truth unreachable by the usual sensory or intellectual means.

- It doesn't last long.

- It feels as if one is not willing or controlling the experience; it includes a sense of a superior presence or power.

- It is a deeply memorable experience, leaving a sense of its importance.

- It changes the inner life of the person who experiences it.

- It changes the outer behavior, attitudes, character, and outlook of the person experiencing it.

We've all had some spiritual experiences of varying intensity and effects. *Déjà vu,* creative inspiration,
intuitive knowledge, and deep love are the everyday
experiences of our spirituality. Intense, even over-
whelming feelings of wonder and appreciation of the
beauty of nature; a sudden jolt of recognition or understanding; a momentary sense of oneness with humanity
and the universe—these are all spiritual experiences.

But these common experiences don't necessarily affect us in a dramatic or long-lasting way. They can be
thought of as flashes or sneak previews of a more
profound and transformational spiritual awakening. For
some of us, a deeply painful experience—some form of
"hitting bottom"—provides the necessary openness to
experiencing a true spiritual awakening.

Linda's Story

Linda describes herself as having been a "wild girl"
during her high school years. "I chose alcohol and drugs
as my stress relievers," she explains. "I had really low
self-esteem, and used booze, pot, LSD, and speed to
feel better. I ran with a real wild crowd, partied all the
time, and my grades in school fell way down. I just
didn't care about anything."

At seventeen, Linda found herself in the hospital with
a fractured skull. She had been out drinking and drugging with her friends all night, and ended up in a car
accident. Facing surgery, all Linda could think about
was the prospect of having her beautiful long hair
shaved off. "I didn't think I was pretty at all," she
remembers, "but I thought my hair was my best feature.
I cried at the thought of losing the one part of my body
I liked. There was a good chance I'd be epileptic for
the rest of my life, or that I'd even die. But I never

thought about that. I didn't care about anything but losing my hair."

After three days in the hospital and numerous tests and x-rays, Linda was scheduled for surgery. The night before her operation, Linda experienced what she calls a "conversion." Alone in her room, she felt herself float out of her body. "It was a very pleasant, peaceful feeling," she says. "I just sort of rested on the ceiling. Sometimes I was in the TV up on the wall too. It was totally different from anything I'd ever experienced— even on drugs. I looked down on myself in the bed, and felt this strong sensation of a voice within me. It said that I could leave or stay, but if I stayed, I couldn't be as I had been before. I felt I was being told that I had certain abilities and I had to start using them, or I wouldn't continue living.

"I felt it would have been totally okay to have crossed over right then and died—I sensed strongly that death is nothing to fear. But I also felt that I was being given a chance to change and to make my life mean something. I was being given a clear choice, one that I hadn't known was available to me until then. I had surgery the next day, and the doctors found blood clots on my brain that hadn't shown up on the CAT scan or EEGs. They kept saying they couldn't believe I was alive. But I knew that I had chosen to live."

Linda stayed in the hospital for several weeks. "Even with my hair shaved off, that iodine-colored stuff they put all over one side of my head, and bandages everywhere, I didn't feel ugly at all. I remember my friends coming to visit me, seeing me like that, and I felt completely peaceful and content, even though I'd lost my hair. It just didn't matter anymore."

Linda says she has never felt a need to tell people about this experience, to have it validated, or to prove it to anyone. "I just *knew* what had happened, and it didn't matter if anyone else knew, or believed me, or understood. I just never doubted it." Along with this sense of certainty that it did happen, Linda also says it gave an "intense purpose" to the rest of her life. "The experience gave me a strong sense that God was in me—that whatever creative abilities I had were part of that *Godness* in me, and I had a responsibility to use them."

Some people might discount this story, and others like it, as drug-, injury-, or withdrawal-induced hallucinations. Whether such stories constitute evidence of God or human spirituality is up to each of us to decide for ourselves. But from a purely pragmatic viewpoint, the value of such experiences cannot be denied. Linda changed her "wild" behavior, stopped abusing drugs and alcohol, and brought her grades up enough to win a college scholarship. She discovered and developed her talents and abilities, and built a successful career helping others. She now says, "I *know* that skull fracture saved my life."

When life gives us inspirational, transformational experiences, we don't have to have documented proof of what caused them or what they mean. We can listen to our own hearts and simply accept them as gifts from God, the positive energy of the universe, or our own highest selves.

Out of the Darkness

Like the man who dreamt he was a butterfly, once we awaken to our spirituality, we can never again be quite sure of ourselves as mere egos. Having opened a window to the light of our spiritual selves, the darkness in our minds can never be quite so dark again.

For most of us, coming to our true spiritual identity doesn't happen suddenly. We have to persist in being open to it and take advantage of all our opportunities for spiritual growth. We do this by patient awareness of the lesson each present moment brings. We do it by accepting where we are right now, today, without anxiety over where we have been or where we are going.

We can help ourselves experience our spirituality through prayer, meditation, and Acting As If—trying to discover the loving part of ourselves by behaving in a loving manner. We can recognize our ego and spirit by their manifestations in our thoughts, actions, and lives. We can use our mind to choose our spirit's viewpoint.

Our deep inner happiness and ability to withstand all the problems and experiences of human life depend on recognizing our true spiritual identity. We are far more than our bodies, desires, mistakes, and behaviors. We are capable of living spiritually, lovingly, peacefully, and happily—even in the world as it is. All we have to change is our minds.

Exercises

Exercise One

Identifying Ego Games. Read through the list of ego games in this chapter (denial, rationalization, blame, competition, complication, projection, attachment, transference, body equals self, and fear). Choose one that seems powerful for you. Find specific examples of it in your attitudes and behavior.

Exercise Two

A Visualization. Imagine you are alone in a beautiful room. This room is your own mind. There are two windows in this room: one looks out on the world from the viewpoint of your ego, and the other through the eyes of your spirit. Remember your ego sees only through fear, anger, blame, and separation; your spirit sees only through love, peace, joy, and oneness.

Now think about a certain relationship or problem you are having. Look at it first through the window of your ego. Just observe your ego's viewpoint. Then turn away from this window and look through the window of your spirit. See the problem in a new way. See love, peace, joy, forgiveness, healing, and joining in the situation. Remember that your mind always has the power to turn from the window of your ego to the window of your spirit.

CHAPTER FOUR

Relationships

In no place is happiness sought more hopefully and dashed more consistently than within relationships, and still we continue to see in them our ultimate delivery from a wilderness of pain.

—Hugh Prather

Relationships with others are an important part of all our lives. They can also be the most problematic part. Many of our problems in relationships are caused by our ego's control issues and desire for self-protection, or our expectations and assumptions about others. We may expect our relationships to provide our happiness and fulfill all of our needs. We may not want to have to work at our relationships, to grow in our understanding and ability to communicate, compromise, and accept others as they are.

Hit and Run

In relationships, Mark calls himself a "hit and runner." He says, "I enter a space, check out all of the people there, see what's happening, make some kind of impact on the space as a whole, and then it's 'Well, gotta go, see you later, bye!' and I breeze back out. Everyone is left saying, 'What happened? Who was that?' And the next time, I just come in and do the same thing. This allows me to be *almost* in relationship with everyone. Then, hopefully, I can pick and choose the people I want to get further involved with."

Mark says he does this to protect himself from being hurt. "I want to see somebody's cards before I get involved in the game," he says. "Unless I'm sure I can invest myself in a person, I don't want to give them the ammunition to shoot at me."

But Mark has found that this attempt at self-protection often hurts himself and others. "I've hurt a lot of people by being *almost* their friend—by acting friendly, but not really being their friend," he says. "It causes a lot of confusion and pain. There's a lot of responsibility in relationships."

We often attempt to avoid our responsibility in relationships by convincing ourselves that we aren't in them. We feel "almost" in relationships, not fully present or participating. We delude ourselves by believing that we aren't really there, so that if anyone gets hurt or things go wrong in some way, we won't feel responsible.

But the truth is that we *are* in relationship with everyone in our lives—even if they're only in our lives for five minutes. We have some responsibility for the nature of every one of our relationships. We choose our own role in these relationships—what we're willing to do, give, and be in them. By being "almost" there, we're choosing not to give of ourselves or to allow others to choose their role in the relationship. We're trying to control the whole thing by ourselves.

Hot and Cold

Another way we avoid commitment and responsibility in our relationships is by repeated advancing and retreating. We send the messages "come here" and "go away" alternately, keeping the other person unsure of us, and the relationship up in the air.

Allen says, "I run hot and cold. I act like I want to be friends, and then I act like I don't, and then I act like I do, and then I act like I don't, and pretty soon people are saying, 'Hey, either you do or you don't!' And they have every right to do that, because it's confusing. It's really a one-sided game where I say, 'This is *my* relationship and I get to make it whatever I want at any given time.' And that's not fair, and it's not a relationship. It's just me doing whatever I want to do. It's not being *in relationship* with someone else."

But Allen *is* in relationship with these people—he's just chosen a very controlling role for himself in them. He's not taking the other person into consideration, or allowing the other person to choose what he or she wants out of the relationship.

Relationships always involve risk. By accepting that we *are* in relationship with others, rather than believing that we can choose to be "almost" or not really in them, we take the risks of rejection, disagreement, separation, and pain. We also take the risks of love, compromise, understanding, and joining with others.

Why are positive elements of relationships such as love and joining with others *risks?* Because we are often as afraid of being liked as we are of *not* being liked. When people show us that they like us, are interested in getting to know us better, we have to decide how to respond and whether we want to move forward with more of ourselves into the relationship. Allen says he runs hot and cold because he's afraid of committing to a relationship. He says, "With some people, particularly women, if they like me a lot, they can be mighty threatening. I feel if I try to make some kind of

43

commitment or be responsible for a portion of a relationship I really care about, maybe I'm going to screw it up."

We can learn, through our relationships, not only to trust, but also to *be trustworthy*. We learn, if we let ourselves, to give and take, forgive and be forgiven, agree and disagree, to understand and to be understood. We learn to accept "screwing it up" a little sometimes, and to learn, grow, and move forward from there. Mistakes don't always have to mean the end of a relationship, and the end of a relationship doesn't have to mean the end of the world.

Relationships can stretch us, teach us, and heal us. We can be hurt in relationships too. And even with the best intentions, we can sometimes hurt others. But *all* of our relationship experiences can help us grow in our understanding of, and love for, ourselves and others.

Family

It's often been said that we can choose our friends, but not our family. Many of us feel that if we could, we would choose very different family relations than the ones we have. Our family relationships are often the most difficult, painful, and complicated of all our relationships.

Our family of origin—the primary group of people we grew up with—taught us a great deal about relationships. If the relationships we experienced and observed as children were difficult, unhappy ones, we often carry these difficulties into other later relationships. And even after we examine our childhood experiences and grow into healthier, happier adult relationships with others, those old family ties may continue to be strained.

For example, just being in the same room with our parents can bring out all the old fear, anger, or sadness of the child who still lives deep inside us. We may find ourselves afraid to state our true feelings or opinions, to disagree with them, to be ourselves. We may allow our parents to treat us as children or as roles they placed us in years ago and never let us out of in their minds.

Forced Roles

Elizabeth was the eldest of four children. She feels that her family assigned her the role of "the good daughter." "The others had their roles," she explains. "There was 'the artistic one,' 'the wild one,' and 'the pretty one.' But I was 'the good one,' 'the *perfect* one'— reliable, responsible, and obedient, a good student who always helped out at home and never gave my family any trouble."

Within her family, this role has stuck with Elizabeth all the way into her forties. "My parents *still* see 'the good daughter' when they look at me," she says. "They don't see *me*. I'm still supposed to help them out and be the reliable, obedient one. My brothers and sister can have all kinds of problems, go off and do whatever they want, and that's okay, but not me. My family won't even accept the fact that I'm a recovering alcoholic."

It's hard for Elizabeth to assert herself with her family. "Whenever I'm around them, I fall back into the old routine," she explains. "I don't disagree with them or explain clearly who I am now or refuse anything they ask of me. I feel confused about my own thoughts, opinions, and identity when I'm with them. Whenever I *have* tried to assert myself with them, they've acted like I've done something terrible against the family. I just feel it's not worth the struggle to fight them."

Elizabeth continues, "Any belief, attitude, decision, or action I've ever taken that wasn't what they would have chosen for me is blamed on my husband. They'd say, 'Elizabeth would never do that,' even though I'd just *done* it! They say my husband is influencing me and taking me away from them. So I don't even try getting through to them anymore. But it makes me feel awful. The only way I seem to be able to be myself is by staying away from them altogether."

Like Elizabeth, many of us were assigned very specific roles in our families. Breaking out of them is a step forward in our personal growth and development. We can examine our family systems and our roles in them, choose the beliefs and behaviors we want to keep, and let go of the rest.

But our families may not be willing to give up their view of us in the old role. They may not be able to see us as we see our adult selves. It may simply be easier for them to blame a spouse, friend, school, job, or city for the changes they can't deny seeing in us. It may be very hard for them to accept the reality that their child grew up and made some choices they wouldn't have made for us or expected us to make for ourselves.

All we can do in this case is try to understand their feeling threatened, and accept that they *can't* see us the way we see ourselves. We can let go of feeling that we need their recognition, acceptance, and approval of us as we are. We can accept our relationship as it is, and choose not to agonize over what it isn't. Maybe someday our family relationships may change, maybe they won't. Either way, we can maintain our own self-image, make our own choices, live our own lives, and know that we are all right, even without the complete understanding of our family.

"The Brady Bunch" Syndrome

Other problems in family relationships occur not because of our expectations of individuals, but because of our idealized image of what a family should be. As long as we harbor fantasies of being "The Brady Bunch" or some other fictional symbol of the perfect family, our own real-life family will seem unsatisfying.

Martha's three grown children live in three different states. Divorced for twenty years, Martha now sees her children and their families once every year or two. "I always had this ideal of the perfect family," she says. "I know I'll never have that white-picket-fence fantasy marriage, but I just don't understand why the rest of us can't seem to be a close, happy, loving family. My children don't call, write, or visit each other. They don't even remember each other on birthdays or holidays. I keep calling to remind them, and ask what's wrong, but it doesn't do any good. They're scattered all over the place, with no communication between them. I just don't understand it. You just don't cut yourself off from your family like that."

As long as Martha's mind is stuck in the belief that she needs to have this image of a close-knit family fulfilled in order to be happy, she'll never be happy. We can't control how other people choose to live their lives—even members of our family. We can't know what's best for them, or make them conform to our ideas of what "you just don't do."

But as soon as we accept reality, we can learn that our happiness doesn't depend on anything other family members think, feel, or do. We can learn to let go of our old fantasies of what our family *should* be, and accept whatever it really *is*.

In-Laws and Remarriage

If we can't choose our families of origin, we also have little control over the families we marry into, or the people who marry into our family. These relationships are frequently strained and can strain the primary relationships in our family.

After Greg's mother died, his fifty-five-year-old father joined a grief support group. There, he met a twenty-four-year-old woman, fell in love, and soon married her. Greg tried hard to be calm and supportive of his father's decision. He adopted a "live and let live" attitude, maintaining a good, open relationship with his father. But other family members let their negative reactions to the news be known in no uncertain terms. Anger and tension spread throughout the family. Friction reigned in what had once been close, happy relationships. Greg says, "It just hasn't been like a family anymore."

Remarriage is often difficult for families to face. New relationships may strain under the weight of old loyalties. Old images of the family and its members must give way to new ones. But if we let go of our attachments to the past and to fantasy images, we can maintain strong family relationships. Then, if the changes turn out well, we can share in our family's joy. If not, we can be a source of love and support, rather than recriminations and "I-told-you-so's."

The same principle applies when any family member brings a new person into our family, or when we have to deal with the family of a lover or spouse. We can't expect to necessarily like all these people, enjoy their company, or have much in common with them. If it happens that we do, that's great. But if not, that can be okay too. Our happiness and inner peace don't depend on what anyone else does, thinks, feels, or who they choose to be with.

When we let go of all our expectations and assumptions, we can be more open to discovering positive feelings toward others. We can accept them as they are, and learn that we don't need them to be any certain way. Conflicts that arise within or because of in-law relationships can be diffused, if not resolved, by simply letting go of our attachments to the past or to fantasy family images. It isn't worth alienating the people we love by judging the people they love.

Children

Sharon waited until she was thirty, established in her career, and married for five years before she decided to have a baby. When her daughter was born, Sharon says she felt "real love" for the first time in her life. "I remember vividly, holding my baby and thinking, *Wow! This is what love is. I've never loved anyone like this before—not even my husband.* I knew right away that it was somehow *different* and special. I loved her more than I ever knew I could love another human being. She's still the only person I've ever loved like that— totally and *unconditionally.*"

This special bond parents feel for their children can be wonderful. It can also make the relationship harder in the sense that everything in it is so important to us. We try to provide our children with everything they need to grow up strong, healthy, smart, safe, and happy. We invest a lot of ourselves in their upbringing. When things go well for our children, we are happy and proud. When things go wrong, we are heartbroken.

We can hardly help but make plans and harbor expectations for our children, and this is where things so often begin to go wrong. Sometimes things just don't work out the way we plan them. All the opportunities we thought we were giving our children may look like burdens, traps, or obligations to them. They may make a lot of the same mistakes we did, no matter what we do or tell them. We want only to spare them every pain, large and small, but children seem to want to rush directly toward the things that may cause them pain.

Sharon says, "I'm convinced, after sixteen years of parenting, that *parents* are the ones who grow up throughout their child's upbringing. I've learned so much about letting go and accepting people and events as they come."

After eight years of lessons, Sharon's daughter gave up playing the piano. Sharon tried not to show it, but her daughter's decision really upset her. "I felt like screaming at her, forcing her to stick with it, telling her she'd regret it later in life. But I did nothing. I told her it was up to her. I told her calmly that I thought she'd do well and be glad if she kept it up, but if she didn't want to, I wouldn't make her. It was the hardest thing I've ever said to her."

Sharon's daughter quit the lessons, and hasn't played the piano since. But Sharon has decided that it's okay. "I gave up my ideas about what she should be and do. I'm letting *her* show me who she is, and I'm finding I like her a lot. I can love her and be proud of her and happy for her, whatever she decides to do."

People are affected by parenting in varying degrees, depending on their own viewpoint, sensitivity, and openness. But within the experience of parenting lies the *opportunity* for unparalleled growth. When we open ourselves to all we can learn from our children, throughout our lives, we ourselves can grow up again and again. When we let go of expecting to find our happiness *through* our children, we discover the happiness of peaceful, loving relationships with them.

Love

Many of us think of our relationships with others on four levels: *love, like, indifference,* and *dislike* or *hate.* Most other people fall into the *indifference* category. These are people we have no real relationship with— either we've never met them or only shared a few unimportant minutes with them.

Most of the people in our daily lives can be divided into *likes* and *dislikes:* co-workers, classmates, acquaintances, some relatives, and friends. We judge them by how they look, what they say and do, the beliefs and attitudes they express, and how they treat us. We may move them back and forth between the *like* and *dislike* categories. Sometimes we turn these *likes* into *dislike* or even *hate* relationships, but what has usually happened is that the person simply stopped filling some need in us. Or perhaps our expectations, fantasies, or assumptions about him or her turned out to be false.

Only a very few people fall into the *love* category. We have all kinds of definitions that add up to what we call "love": admiration, affection, trust, respect, concern, loyalty, intimacy, and attraction, to name but a few. There is also an element of *specialness* in what we call a love relationship, something that makes it *exclusive* in some way. This can be something like shared secrets, sexual fidelity, or family ties. Or it can be something less tangible and more difficult to define.

One man says, "Real love is about very particular people. No one else can fill that mold. It's not like being 'in love,' where you're happy because you're getting certain needs and desires met—which lots of other people could probably meet just as well. Real love is very focused on that specific individual."

Sometimes we define love as an action rather than a feeling. One woman says, "It's caring for another's well-being and what you can add to that." Sometimes what we call "love" crosses over into dependency, addiction, or even obsession. We divide love into types, such as *platonic, maternal,* or *romantic.* We indulge in great philosophical debates about what love really is and how many people we can share it with. As much as we want it, talk about it, sing about it, and write about it, and as important as it is to us, we still seem pretty confused about love.

"Love all, trust a few."

There is another way of looking at this whole issue of love and relationships. We can *simplify* our very complicated viewpoint. First, we can eliminate the *dislike or hate* and *indifference* categories altogether. The only purpose they serve is to delude our egos into believing that we can choose not to be in relationships with some others, or that we can protect ourselves by judging and holding grievances against some people.

Obviously, we can't interact directly with everyone else in the world, but we *are* in relationship with them, all the time. We share the planet, and affect each other in many ways we may not realize. We also can't like everyone, condone their behavior, or enjoy their company, but we *can* stop judging them and holding grievances against them. Once we've eliminated these two negative categories, we can concentrate on the two positive ones.

William Shakespeare wrote, "Love all, trust a few." We can love all others by accepting them as they are and wishing them only peace, joy, and healing of mind, heart, and body. This does not mean foolish acceptance of abuse or harm in any way. As Hugh Prather writes, "Opening one's heart does not imply opening one's house, one's purse, one's front door, or any other action. Being a component of happiness, acceptance is purely mental." The acceptance and forgiveness required to "love all" are *attitudes,* not actions. But the attitudes of loving all will manifest in our own inner peace, happiness, and outer responsibility toward others.

This new kind of love is universal, unconditional, and *inclusive* rather than exclusive. It means valuing peace and understanding over conflict and grievances. It means trying to relate to others on the level of our spirits and theirs, instead of communicating only on the level of our egos. It means openness, acceptance, and forgiveness.

Forgiveness

Forgiveness is a key element in universal, unconditional love. We can practice it in many ways, and in *all* of our relationships. We can begin with small exercises in forgiving those with whom we have seemingly unimportant relationships.

Lucie tells us of her experiment in forgiveness: "My husband and I frequently order pizza from a local restaurant that delivers," she says. "They have this deal where your order gets to your house within thirty minutes or you get a discount. We always set our kitchen timer as soon as we called in the order, and then usually, the guy would just be pulling up as the timer went off. But once, the timer rang and he still wasn't there.

"While we waited, we talked about the discount and whether or not we should demand it. We had been talking about forgiveness and trying to incorporate it into our lives. This seemed like a perfect opportunity to practice it. We decided not to mention it and pay the full price. We had the money set aside already, anyway, so it was no big deal. We even wondered if the driver would mention it himself, since the time of the call was always clearly marked on the box.

"The pizza man came almost ten minutes late, said nothing about it, and we paid the full price—we even tipped him as usual. But my husband and I didn't feel angry or cheated at all. In fact, we felt *great* all evening—as if we had done some kind of good deed. We had chosen to see being right as less important than being calm, peaceful, and happy. Interestingly, we have ordered pizza from the same place many times since, and it always arrives within fifteen minutes!"

Such small exercises in forgiveness can teach us how easy it is to let go of so many of our daily grievances. The truth is, they just don't matter that much. But what about the big things? What about the things that really do matter and affect our lives dramatically? How can we forgive the real tragedies and atrocities that fill our world?

Forgiveness is not easy in these cases because they trigger our ego's attachment to fear, anger, and retribution. Of course, our law enforcement and criminal justice systems are necessary to protect innocent people. And we have a right and responsibility to end relationships with people who harm us. But in our hearts and minds, we can wish for these perpetrators healing and peace, rather than vengeance. Anger, fear, and retaliation can never undo a harm once it's done, but they can harm us.

Forgiveness is for ourselves, not for those against whom we hold grievances. It frees us of our own self-poisoning anger and fear. It clears out the negative feelings and attitudes in our minds, making room for the positive ones. We don't have to have anything to do with the people we forgive directly. All we have to do is let go of our own attachment to feelings of anger, fear, and vengeance.

Regular, small exercises in forgiveness—like Lucie's story of the pizza delivery—can help us get in practice for letting go of our bigger grievances. We can make a habit of forgiveness, so that it comes more quickly and naturally to us.

In *The Power of Your Subconscious Mind,* Joseph Murphy writes that the "acid test" for forgiveness is how you feel when you hear some wonderful news about someone who's hurt you in the past. If you feel any negative reaction, you have not yet fully forgiven. When you hear the good news and you are unaffected, "psychologically and spiritually," then you have truly forgiven. This state of mind frees us to find true happiness within ourselves.

Special Relationships

"Trust a few" is generally what we do already, even if we don't call it that. These are our special relationships: the people we like, admire, enjoy, and connect with on some level. We choose to be around certain people because they fill certain needs in us.

These relationships can last any length of time, depending on circumstances and our changing needs. For example, a college roommate may be the closest person to us for a few years, and then, after graduation, we may never see that person again. People we date, work with, go to school with, or live near, come and go throughout our lives.

Some of our "likes" are very strong and we call them "love." They make us feel safe, accepted, understood, and important. They are *exciting* relationships—sexually, mentally, or emotionally stimulating and satisfying. We want them to last forever. Or rather, we want that *feeling* to last forever.

But again, we change, our needs change, other people change, and so our relationships change too. That wonderful feeling we wanted to last forever never does. This reality may leave us feeling disappointed or even despairing. We may become angry or blaming toward the other person. We may begin looking for someone else who will be the "right" person, or we may withdraw from close relationships to avoid experiencing the pain of separation again.

The trouble here is caused by our insistence on making our happiness dependent on our "love" relationships. As Jerry Jampolsky writes, "Every time I hand over to another person the power to determine my happiness, I will end up in agony and conflict." If we concentrate on. our own inner peace and happiness instead, we can try to love all, and *like* a few. All of our "like" relationships can then be seen as enriching experiences, regardless of their intensity, length, or outcome.

Our delusions and fantasies about love reveal themselves to be false again and again. But when we hold on to them like drowning people clinging to a lifeboat, we've forgotten that if we just relax and let go, we can float *all by ourselves*.

Being Alone

It is natural for human beings to be drawn together. We organize ourselves into nations, cities, neighborhoods, and families. We create groups based on our shared interests, goals, hobbies, careers, beliefs, and problems. We fill our lives with relationships of varying intensity and purpose.

I believe humans are attracted to each other because we sense, perhaps unconsciously, that on a deep, spiritual level, we are all one. We are naturally drawn to joining together because this oneness is our natural state. But because our peace, happiness, and spirituality are found deep within ourselves, we can experience them in solitude, and often *need* to.

When Anna's unhappy marriage broke up, she felt the need to be alone for a while. Invited to spend Christmas Eve and Christmas Day with friends, she chose instead to stay at home, completely alone. "I was happy when my husband moved out at Thanksgiving, but I felt a little strange about spending Christmas alone," she tells us. "Still, I felt I *needed* to do it somehow."

This time of solitude turned out to be what Anna calls "a special time that completely changed my life." Instead of feeling lonely or frightened, Anna says, "All of a sudden I felt the whole house was *full*—full of spirit, of life and love, and a strong sense of peace. I suddenly felt more *secure* than I had ever felt before. I knew I'd always be all right, no matter what. I felt a strong spiritual connection to something outside myself— something much, much bigger. I suddenly understood that my security wasn't contingent upon anything but this connection. I knew that no matter what happened,

I'd still have this spiritual connection, and I'd be all right."

We all need some time to be alone, to observe our own thoughts, to get to know ourselves, and perhaps to discover, as Anna did, our spirituality. Sometimes we need to withdraw from relationships for a while in order to rest, heal, and grow. Sometimes we need to let new beliefs, attitudes, and behaviors "sink in" and solidify within ourselves for a time before we can begin practicing them with others.

Ted, who lives alone, calls himself a "basically isolate person." A recovering alcoholic and drug addict, he says, "People now make jokes about my being 'antisocial.' I used to be *so* social—'social' is hardly the word for it. I used to live my life through other people and drugs and alcohol. I think I went through a period of being extremely afraid of socializing because I felt I would lapse into the same patterns again. I also felt for a time that there was a part of this whole recovery thing that was mine and mine alone, and I was busy experiencing that. So I just stayed away from other people."

Ted has now been recovering for several years, and no longer fears socializing with other people. He has learned to balance time spent with others and time alone. He says, "Now I find that I go out and spend a lot of time with a lot of people, and then I need to go and be alone to reflect. I spend a lot of time going over things in my mind—how I have acted and how other people have acted. I ask a lot of 'Why?' questions in my mind about things—like, *Why did this happen the way it did, and what do I feel about it, and what do I want to do about it now?* I really need my time alone to do all that."

Our time alone can be filled with healthy, helpful introspection, meditation, or prayer. It can be a wonderful opportunity to take a break from our personal and social relationships, to gain perspective, and to grow closer to ourselves and our Higher Power. We can use this time to clarify our thoughts and feelings, refresh our contact with our spirituality, and come back to our relationships with more to share.

Loneliness

Sometimes being alone doesn't feel so good. We may feel that we don't have the kinds or numbers of relationships we'd like. This time alone may sometimes feel more painful than spiritual, more lonely than replenishing.

Ted says he learned more about his need for others during his time alone. "A part of your spirituality is what you are sharing with other people's spirituality," he says. "I believe there is spirituality in aloneness and in meditation, but it's necessary that someone else's spirit be there in order to exercise a certain part of your spirituality." We long to exercise this part of our spirituality, to join with others lovingly and peacefully.

When we focus on our own well-being, growth, and spirituality, and find positive ways to spend our time, relationships will make themselves available to us. For example, volunteer work is often a great way to meet people with similar interests and make a contribution to our community at the same time. Hospitals, food banks, libraries, community centers, and political campaigns always need volunteers. Amateur theatre and musical groups, church organizations, and special interest clubs are available in every community. And a wide variety of classes are offered at low cost or even free at many schools, community centers, and libraries.

Support groups are available if we want to talk with other people who have similar problems. There are groups for alcohol, drug, sex, and gambling addictions, eating disorders, chronic illnesses, and grief. There are groups for parents and single parents, and divorced or widowed people. There is a group for everyone who wants one. All we have to do is get out and look for the one that's right for us—and if we don't like the first one we go to, we can try another one.

We may sabotage our chances at wonderful experiences if we set our minds on specific expectations of people or relationships. Strategies for finding friends and mates are doomed to failure. Desperate desire for someone to be with can lead to impulsive intimacy and ultimate misery. Friendships form when common interests bring us together first.

Relationships will unfold if we let them. But we have to concentrate on our own growth and development, our own spirituality, and our own relationship with ourselves *first*. When we use our time alone well, we gradually become ready to reach out into the world with ourselves to share. Then, others will appear and share themselves with us.

Endings and Beginnings

Relationships, like people; are constantly changing. They may grow closer, warmer, happier, healthier, deeper, stronger, and more satisfying. They may also grow weaker, cooler, and more distant. All of these changes require us to re-evaluate and adjust our view of the relationships and our part in them.

Endings often give us the most trouble. We have created something that filled up a certain space in our lives, and without it, we have to do a lot of rearranging of ourselves, our time, and perhaps, our place of work or home. We also have to adjust our self-image without the relationship. On top of all that, we have to sort out our feelings about the other person and the way the relationship developed and ended. If this all sounds like hard work, it usually is. But it is also one of the greatest opportunities for personal growth we can experience.

Rick tells us that "the end of a love experience" was one of the hardest things he's ever lived through. "The hardest thing about it was my battle with myself to understand that I couldn't undo what had happened to the relationship," he says. "It was winding down into nothing but a big problem, and I couldn't change it. I wanted and tried desperately to get back what we'd had when the relationship was brand new."

Rick continues, "When the relationship finally ended, I was full of a lot of self-pity. I felt *I* had worked so hard, and *I* had done this and *I* had done that, and yet the relationship wasn't going anywhere." After a period of feeling bitter, Rick began to realize how controlling he had been in the relationship. He says, "I learned to be more sensitive to the input other people are giving me, and not to make nearly as many assumptions about relationships as I had."

Being open to learning about our own mistakes in relationships, rather than blaming others, can make these experiences extremely valuable to us. If we let go of our fear, pride, anger, and our ego's delusion of self-protection, we can learn many important lessons. We can take the time we need to *grow through* the experience instead of just trying to survive it.

Time helped Rick to gain distance and perspective. He says, "It allowed me to see the smallness of the time we'd spent together in terms of my entire life, and how much more of my life was still coming. It became a learning experience rather than something which stopped me from progressing. Eventually, there came a time when I felt that that relationship, that part of my life, was *okay*. It didn't work—or rather, it *did* work, it was what it was—and it was okay. I didn't have to grieve it continually for the rest of my life."

Rick's difficult experience gave him insight, acceptance, and hope for better relationships in the future. He gained tremendous understanding which he may not have found any other way. Our relationship problems and endings can teach us and help us grow, if we let them. Even if they hurt for a while, we can gain much more than we lose in them.

Endings clear the way for new beginnings. After we have learned what we can from these experiences, we let them go to make space in our minds, hearts, and lives for new relationships. We can't move on to new experiences as long as we cling stubbornly to old pain or even fond memories. We have to accept endings inside ourselves before we can progress outwardly.

New beginnings are exciting. They awaken us with fresh feelings, thoughts, and experiences. If we bring everything we have learned to them, they can be better than anything we've experienced in the past. Each new beginning is a chance to discover more about ourselves and others, to stretch ourselves in new ways, to learn how much we have to give and how much others can give to us.

When we let go of our desire for control, our expectations and assumptions, and our ego's wish for self-protection, we can open ourselves to wonderful new relationships. We can join with others in love and peace. We can experience our spiritual oneness with all other human beings and our Higher Power. We can fill our lives with happy, healthy relationships.

Exercises

Exercise One

Family Roles. What was the role you filled in your family? Was there a label that went along with it? How do you feel about the role now? Do you still try to fill it with members of your family? With others? What parts of the role do you like and want to keep? Which parts would you like to shed? How can you begin?

Exercise Two

Fantasy Images. What are your images of an ideal family? An ideal love relationship? An ideal friendship? What are your expectations of others within these images? Do others usually fulfill your expectations? How do you feel when they don't? Can you see any ways in which you try to control others or relationships? What would happen if you gave up all your fantasies and expectations of others? Try it in one specific relationship and see what really does happen.

Exercise Three

Forgiveness. This exercise has two parts: taking a forgiving attitude and a forgiving action. First, think about someone who you feel has hurt you in some way. Decide in your mind to let the grievance go. Now hold the image of this person in your mind, and ask your spirit and your Higher Power to show you what they see in this person. Ask for a new way of seeing your relationship. Second, perform some small act of forgiveness. This can be something like Lucie's late pizza delivery story. Realize that it just doesn't matter. You are fine without the anger and sense of righteousness you are giving up—in fact, it feels like a great weight being lifted from you.

Exercise Four

Being Alone. Take time to be alone with yourself every day. Turn off the TV, radio, and any other distractions. Just spend some time with *you,* getting to know your own thoughts and feelings. Try to find the most loving, peaceful part of yourself. Enjoy this time and make it a regular part of your day.

CHAPTER FIVE

Other People's Problems

Other people do not have to change for us to experience peace of mind.

—Jerry Jampolsky

Other people's problems can affect us in many ways, creating a real challenge to our serenity, our balance, or equanimity. If we allow our ego-responses to be triggered, we may find ourselves reacting to other people's problems with guilt, anger, worry, fear, or some other form of defensiveness. We may feel responsible for fixing whatever's wrong, or guilty because we can't. We may get caught on our ego's treadmill of attack and defend.

Miranda and Her Mother

Miranda says her life goes along pretty well most of the time. She has a happy marriage, work she loves, a new house, and generally feels content. But when Miranda talks with her mother on the phone, everything changes. "I get so worried about her," Miranda tells us. "She's widowed, lives alone in another city, and because of a physical handicap, can't get a job or drive a car. She absolutely refuses to sell her house and move closer to me. When my father's pension benefits ran out, I went crazy with worry. Luckily, I was in a position to start sending her some money every month, but it's never enough. She still talks constantly about how poor she is. I don't know what else I can do."

Miranda says she thinks about her mother's problems a lot of the time. "I feel like my self-image as a good person rests on how well I take care of her," she says. "I do what I can, but I can't take care of her emotions. I feel attacked by her continued griping, even though I *am* sending her money and calling her all the time."

Even though Miranda knows she is doing all she can, and the money she sends her mother really does help, she still feels guilty, worried, and angry whenever she talks with her mother. "The guilt and worry come in a long list of 'What if . . .' fantasies," she says. "The anger comes from *knowing* I'm not responsible for her happiness and yet *feeling* somehow that I am."

Beyond Caring

Whenever we move beyond caring and compassion to actually trying to fix someone else's problems, we get caught in a battle of egos. We feel attacked by another's lack of serenity, his or her unhappiness, and the reality of his or her problems. The person may feel attacked by the problem, our attempt to help, or our inability to succeed at it. We may both feel defensive and resentful.

We cannot take care of ourselves, our true happiness, peace of mind, and well-being, while we are trying to control someone else's life, problems, or feelings. We can't make another person happy, and we don't need his or her happiness in order to find our own. If we remember that happiness—our highest well-being—comes from within each of us, we can see that all our outer manipulations are futile.

When we recognize our ego's defensive response to other people's problems, we can begin turning to our spirit for another point of view. Our spirit's viewpoint is loving and giving, but not in an obsessive, controlling, or guilt-driven way. It is also as loving toward ourselves as it is toward others. In some relationships, such as that of parents and grown children, we may be particularly prone to our ego's viewpoint rather than our spirit's.

Adult Children

As our parents age, we may feel that we owe them something. After all, they raised us and possibly sacrificed for us in some ways. Like Miranda, we may feel somehow responsible for their happiness and well-being. But we must carefully examine what we realistically can and can't do for them.

We can, as Miranda did, help them out financially, if it is possible for us to do so. We can drive them to the store or to doctor's appointments if we have the time and live close enough to them. We can call or visit them occasionally to see how they are and let them know we care about them. Sometimes we may be able to do small but important things for them, such as moving heavy furniture.

Often, we can help our parents in such concrete ways as getting them the help they need, but we can never take care of or control their feelings. If we call or visit regularly, they may still feel lonely. If we get them the best medical care available, they may complain, mistrust the doctors and nurses, refuse treatment, or even accuse us of not caring about them. In every case, their feelings are within *their* power to choose. We can't control those feelings by any of our actions.

Trying to Win Our Parents' Love

Sometimes we may, perhaps unconsciously, try to get something from our parents we needed as children and didn't get from them. We may do this by adjusting ourselves constantly for them in an attempt to gain their love or avoid their disapproval.

When he married, Alex began realizing how much of his time had been spent doing things for his parents. His new wife was surprised when he'd drop everything and rush over to their house whenever they called. "My parents would call every time some old family friend happened to be in town, and I was expected to go over and socialize with that person, even if I didn't know who he or she was," Alex says. "It never occurred to me to say no until my wife started getting mad because I'd mess up plans she and I had already made. Sometimes I'd leave her alone with guests at our house to go over to my parents'. Sometimes I'd interrupt a quiet evening alone with her because they called and asked me to do something for them. My wife couldn't understand why I treated every request or invitation from my family like a 'command performance.' When her family called, she'd often say, 'Sorry, I'm busy' without thinking twice. I always felt far too guilty to do anything like that."

Examining his feelings toward his aging parents, Alex realized that he feared they might become seriously ill or even die without ever giving him the unconditional love and approval he'd always wanted from them. He couldn't refuse anything they asked of him as long as he believed he could someday gain that approval by complying.

This need we feel for our parents' approval comes from our ego's vulnerable self-image and fear of abandonment. Our ego feels attacked by any sign of disapproval, disagreement, or distress—particularly from our parents. We become defensive of our self-image, our lovability, or even our safety. Our ego may feel threatened for its very life if our parents seem to reject us in some way.

Whether our parents become ill or not has nothing to do with our taking care of ourselves, even if they don't approve of the ways we choose to do that. We can't make them give us what we wanted from them as children and never got. We *can* let go of feeling responsible for their health, happiness, and well-being.

Guilt and Shame

As adults, we may find ourselves replaying other relationship problems from childhood. For example, our relationships with brothers and sisters can affect the way we perceive and react to other people's problems in adulthood.

Rhonda says she finds herself "playing dumb" a great deal, trying to make others feel smarter than herself. She feels guilty for knowing an answer when others seem stumped. She says guilt and shame consume her whenever she achieves a goal or receives some kind of recognition for success in any area of her life. She also feels angry for being unable to enjoy her successes, and angry when others ignore or trivialize her accomplishments. In examining her family of origin, Rhonda began understanding where these feelings came from.

"My brother had a learning disability," she explains. "Back then there weren't all the special programs and help available for these kinds of problems that there are now. It was just sort of whispered around my family that he was a bit 'slow.' We were always supposed to be very careful not to make him feel stupid or bad about himself. That meant that when I got A's, no one paid much attention, but when he got C's, everyone praised him up and down."

Rhonda learned to downplay her academic successes and even to feel guilty for them. "I felt bad because school came easily to me," she says. "I didn't enter contests or apply for scholarships I knew I could win. I turned down some prestigious private colleges, and went to a nearby public university without much fanfare, even though I was the first person in my family to even go to college at all. When I made the dean's list, I didn't tell anyone. I actually felt ashamed of it."

As an adult, Rhonda now says she takes other people's problems as a sign for her to feel guilty and ashamed. "I feel responsible for other people feeling happy and good about themselves," she says, "and I guess deep inside I think that means that I can't feel good about myself."

Guilt for Success

Many of us may feel guilty for our success or lack of problems in certain areas of our lives. If we grew up with a family member who had a particular handicap that required a great deal of the family's time, money, and attention, we may have secretly resented it and consequently felt guilty. Having a special ability, talent, or interest in an area of someone else's weakness may then create guilt or shame in us.

This guilt or shame is created by our ego in response to feeling attacked by another's misfortune. Why would we feel "attacked" by other people's problems? Because *our self-image as a good person may be shaken by being better off than someone else*. Remember, our ego only knows attack and defend. These are its responses to *everything*, even good things that happen to us, and even if it means attacking ourselves with negative feelings such as guilt and shame.

Our ego can create guilt and fear of loss when we acquire something new we aren't used to having or that others still don't have. Peter is a successful businessman who has become quite wealthy by working hard and learning a great deal about investments. He has been careful to make all of his money in the most strictly legal and ethical ways. But he says he still feels guilty for his success and wealth. "I come from a relatively poor family," he says. "We never had more than the bare essentials, and even that was sometimes hard to come by."

Peter says he still feels guilty because there is poverty in the world. "I know no matter what I do, I can't fix that," he says. "I can't feed all the hungry people, and that really makes me feel bad sometimes." Even though Peter helps out his family and contributes generously to charity, he says he fears that his having money somehow deprives others. "I know that's not true," he explains. "I *know* it, but I don't *feel* it. What I feel is responsible for *everybody*. Why should I have any more than anybody else?"

Many recovering alcoholics, drug addicts, and codependents also feel this same kind of guilt. How can we enjoy our newfound health and happiness while other people still suffer? How can life become good for us and still be so awful for others? As long as other people are suffering somewhere, in some way, how can we be happy without at least feeling bad about it?

We Can't Share What We Don't Have

Guilt, fear, and shame do not make us good people. They are merely games our egos play to keep us stuck in unhappiness. They hide the pure joy of our spirit behind the attack and defense of our ego. As Jerry Jampolsky writes, "Guilt and fear cannot coexist with love." But we can let them go and replace them with love, peace, acceptance, and joy.

We find our goodness inside our true selves, our spirits—not in guilt, shame, or self-denial. We live gently, generously, and lovingly when we live guided by our spiritual wisdom, rather than our ego's fear. Our guilt and shame don't alleviate anyone else's problems, they just create problems for ourselves.

We must remember that we can only share love, peace, abundance, joy, understanding, and forgiveness with others when we are in touch with those qualities within ourselves. They are always available to each of us at the level of our spirit. But negative viewpoints such as guilt and shame keep us focused on the level of our ego, which is incapable of them. *Our own spiritual growth and well-being are what enable us to truly help and love others.*

Worry

Worrying gives us the illusion that we are actually doing something to solve a problem or prevent a harm. In reality, all we are doing is revving up our anxiety level and creating negative stress within ourselves. It's like spinning our wheels in sand—there seems to be a lot going on, but we're not going anywhere. Worry is great fun for our egos, and complete nonsense to our spirits.

We may worry about everything from our spouse's job to the world economy. We may worry about our neighbor's children or a war in some faraway country. We may worry about terrible things that have never happened and will never happen. We may worry about what everyone else should and shouldn't be thinking, feeling, wanting, having, or doing.

When we worry about other people's problems, we're neglecting to trust them and their Higher Power to handle things. We're turning away from our spirit's natural hope and faith, and instead, exercising our ego's futile attempt to control other people and events. We are also avoiding constructive thinking about ourselves and our own problems. Worry is truly a waste of time and energy, but it is often our response to other people's problems. We may imagine everything that could possibly go wrong for our parents, children, spouse, lover, friends, and co-workers. We may feel that all this worry helps them somehow, or at least proves we care about them. We may believe that our worrying is natural and out of our control.

We can learn to recognize the difference between caring and ineffective worrying. We can let go of anxious thoughts about what might happen to those we love, and focus our attention on the real choices and problems we have to face. We can let go of our ego's fear and replace it with our spirit's faith, hope, love, and trust.

Marriage

Marriage and other committed relationships can be especially prone to confusion about the question of personal boundaries. If "what's mine is yours, and what's yours is mine," does that include problems? Is our spouse's problem at work *our* problem? Are we responsible for our lover's addictions, relationships with others, or health and happiness?

The closeness of these relationships can make us feel involved in every aspect of each other's lives. But there is a difference between caring or sharing, and feeling responsible. We can share our feelings, give each other a safe place to talk, and try to understand and support each other. But we can't solve each other's problems or control each other's choices and feelings.

The Overprotective Spouse

Ben and his wife, Rosemary, decided early in their relationship not to have children, but to devote their lives to their careers. "Rosemary is really wrapped up in her work, and comes home every night full of stories about things that have happened at the office and decisions she has to make," Ben tells us. "I really am interested in what she does, thinks, and feels. So when she talks to me about her work, I tend to jump right in with my opinions and advice. Sometimes, I give advice that I think can help her. Other times, when someone has treated her badly, I get really mad and I want to call them up, but Rosemary stops me. She gets mad at me for getting so involved in everything she tells me. I just don't get it. Doesn't she want me to be concerned and interested?"

Rosemary says that Ben doesn't really listen to what she says, but just reacts to it. "When I come home from a long day at the office, I want someone to talk to, not someone to solve all my problems for me," she explains. "I don't need a protector or adviser, I need a friend, a lover, a husband. Sometimes I need to hear myself think out loud. Sometimes I need to blow off some steam. Sometimes I just need to share what I'm feeling with someone I can trust. If I wanted help or advice, I'd ask for it."

The thoughts and feelings our lovers and spouses share with us are *gifts*. They're the jewels of closeness and intimacy. If we try to control them, we're betraying that intimacy. We're taking something away from the person we love. We're seeing them as something less than whole, complete, responsible individuals. We may even destroy our relationships.

Rosemary says she doesn't trust Ben with her thoughts and feelings anymore. She says, "If I can't tell him things without having him judge everything I say, tell me what I should do, or even go and talk to someone else about them, then I just can't tell him things anymore." But if Ben accepts the things Rosemary shares with him, listens to her fully and without judgments, and lets go of trying to control her and her life, they can rebuild the trust in their relationship.

The people we love don't need us to rescue them. They don't need our interference or control. They don't need us to take care of their feelings, choices, or actions. They need our attention, respect, support, and acceptance. They need us to listen to them, and to hug them when they're happy as well as when they're sad. They need us to just love them.

Boundaries at Work

Our families and love relationships are not the only places where we allow ourselves to be affected by other people's problems. At work, we often involve ourselves in others' problems by doing extra work for them, listening to (and becoming upset by) their complaints, or even tolerating their abuse.

Our true responsibilities are often more clearly defined at work than anywhere else in our lives. Taking on other people's problems at work can only damage our ability to carry out our own responsibilities, and fill us with anger and resentment. But work may be the place where we feel we have the least power to say no. We may feel defensive about losing our job or our image as a good worker, so we're willing to take on extra responsibility and get along with others.

Setting some boundaries is as necessary at work as it is anyplace else in our lives. If we feel abused in our jobs, we have to make some decisions about what we're willing to give away for the job. Our serenity? Our self-respect? Our peace of mind and true happiness? If we choose not to leave the job itself, we have to decide how we're going to protect these aspects of ourselves.

Our serenity and peace of mind are within us. We can choose to keep them intact despite other people's behavior or problems. But it takes some effort to let go of our ego's feeling attacked by these people and their problems, and turn to our spirit's viewpoint of serenity. This peaceful viewpoint doesn't mean taking the abuse of others or taking on their problems. It means recognizing that their problems are not ours and we can be just fine without trying to solve them or letting them harm us.

Whose Problem Is It, Anyway?

When we examine our attitudes and behavior toward other people's problems, we must always ask ourselves: *Whose problem is it? Who really has the right, responsibility, and power to make this choice?*

It is neither irresponsible nor cruel to expect other people to handle their own problems. It isn't selfish or inconsiderate to concentrate on handling our own. But sometimes it is difficult to wade through all the ego-nonsense and arrive at a clear distinction of exactly who a problem belongs to. This is often because some problems cause others, and then we become confused as to which problem, if any, is ours.

Part of the difficulty comes from our ego's desire to *blame*. We can get bogged down in thinking about who seems to have *caused* the problems, rather than who is responsible for dealing with them *now*. Blaming others for creating our problems doesn't get them resolved. If someone else's choices are causing problems for us, we must sort out which problems are ours to handle.

For example, if someone has an active addiction, that is *their* problem, even if they are someone we love. They are really the only person who can choose what to do about that addiction. But if they abuse us in any way, or if their addiction has any other adverse effects on us, it is *our* problem to decide what we need to do about taking care of ourselves. In this case, trying to cure or control the addiction is overstepping the boundaries of our responsibility; getting out of an abusive relationship or getting help for ourselves is not.

People affected by other people's addictions must let go of taking care of the other person and learn to take care of themselves, but this is also true of *all* our relationships. We must:

- sort through all of the problems or choices to discover which really are *not* ours,

- let them go, and

- focus our attention and effort on those problems that are ours to resolve, or decisions that are ours to make.

Taking Care of Ourselves

Living from our spirits rather than our egos does not mean taking on everyone else's problems. We don't have to "keep the peace" in order to have peace of mind. We can still assert ourselves, respect ourselves, and take care of ourselves in whatever ways truly enhance our well-being and real happiness. If this still strikes us as "selfish," we need to remember that our true happiness and well-being grow out of peaceful relationships, loving ourselves and others, and letting go of our ego's fears.

Loving relationships do not require worrying about or trying to solve the other person's problems. If we see this as a normal part of love, perhaps we are confusing love with projection. Perhaps we see what another person should do because it is something we need to do in our own lives. Perhaps we fear facing our own problems, so we allow our egos to convince us that taking on another's can help us avoid our problems and make us a good person at the same time.

The trouble is, whatever our own problems are, they don't go away because we're not paying attention to them. In fact, they usually get worse. Our ego may persuade us that if someone really loved us, they'd take on our problems and solve them for us. But the end result of all this confusion is simply that *we fail at solving other people's problems for them, and our own problems don't get resolved by our neglect.*

This doesn't mean we can never help or be helped. But love also doesn't mean, "I'll solve your problems and you solve mine." Loving another means, "I'll respect, support, care about you, and help you if I can, but I can't take care of your feelings, choices, or problems." Loving ourselves means, "I'm responsible for my own feelings, choices, and problems, and getting the help I need."

Peace of Mind in a World of Problems

Everybody has problems. We all bump into other people and their problems as we go about our daily lives. Sometimes, thanks to modern mass media, we learn about all kinds of problems of all kinds of people we will never meet or have anything to do with. As Hugh Prather writes, "We get a steady picture of the world ever fretting and wringing its hands."

How do we figure out which problems we really can do something about and which ones are best left to others? How do we protect ourselves from allowing other people's problems, decisions, and lack of serenity to affect us? Sometimes other people attack us directly with their problems, sometimes we may seem to go around looking for problems to latch on to, and sometimes we just happen to find ourselves sharing space with someone who is expressing or "acting out" a problem. This could be any kind of problem, but one common problem we allow ourselves to be affected by is other people's lack of serenity.

Katherine's Loss of Peacefulness

Katherine grew up in a very religious community. She attended Catholic schools, where she says, "All the little girls wanted to grow up to be nuns, and all the little boys wanted to grow up to be priests." The devotion of these children was genuine and innocent. "I was really into the whole thing," Katherine remembers. "I'd come out of mass feeling such a deep spiritual peace and closeness to God."

One summer Sunday, after mass, Katherine came out of the church with her family. "Usually, I stayed up in the choir loft singing until everyone had pretty much dispersed. But that day, I sat with my family because I had a sore throat and couldn't sing. I walked down the church steps to the sidewalk where people were milling about talking in small groups. There were these women who were all dressed up in really fancy clothes and hats—they were the ladies of the congregation we girls were supposed to look up to, the wives and mothers and church volunteers—and I heard them talking about all the other people. It was like, *'Oh, did you see so-and-so? Can you believe what she was wearing? Oh, I know! And she always goes right up to sit in the front so everyone can see her. Really! Having another baby at her age! You know her first daughter got pregnant in high school. . . . '* My peacefulness and serenity were shattered on the spot. I crashed back down to the everyday world of spiteful, back-stabbing, petty gossip. I went home and cried. I'll never forget it."

Katherine remembers this incident so vividly because it was the first time she recalls being affected by someone else's lack of peace and serenity. As a young girl, it was shocking to her that people could come out of church where they'd just been praying and singing about God, love, joy, and peace, and start right in on hurtful gossiping. The experience marked a loss of innocence for Katherine, a realization that not everyone felt as close to God as she did in church, and that people didn't always live up to what they preached and prayed for.

We adults already know these things. We've had enough experience to know that the world and people aren't perfect. But rather than accepting it and maintaining our peacefulness anyway, we often allow others' ego games to pull us out of our serenity. We allow ourselves to react with fear, anger, disappointment, and even despair when we are once again reminded of other people's problems.

The Time to Be Happy Is Now

We cannot put off finding and maintaining our true inner peace and serenity. There will never come a perfect, easy time to do it. We'll be waiting *forever* if we want a world where no one ever has a bad mood or expects us to fix their problems. Instead of waiting for a perfect world, we can help the world move a little closer to that ideal by taking care of our own beliefs, attitudes, and behaviors. We can make a loving, caring contribution to the world's peace and serenity by maintaining our own.

We don't have to resolve other people's problems, or even all the problems that crop up between us and others. But we do have to resolve our feelings about them. For example, if we don't like the way our parents still treat us, we don't have to sit down and iron out an agreement with them about how our relationship with them will change. That may or may not be possible, depending on many factors, and at least partly on *their* choices. But we do have to look at *our* feelings carefully and honestly, and resolve them. Then we can make some decisions about what we need to do to take care of ourselves and our peace, happiness, and well-being.

Carelessly venting our anger toward others is *not* taking care of ourselves or promoting our peace, happiness, or well-being. Even calmly stating how we feel may or may not be truly heard and understood by others. People often hear and see what they want to. They may block out any understanding of what we're expressing. All we can do is let go of other people's beliefs, thoughts, feelings, and actions, and remember to confine our efforts to resolving our own.

How other people's problems affect us is always our choice. If we examine our beliefs, attitudes, and actions *pragmatically,* we can choose the ones that help us and promote our own true health, happiness, and well-being. We can learn to view other people's problems with love and detachment. We can help them in healthy, peaceful ways, and let go of trying to accomplish the impossible. We can trust others to deal with all that is out of our control and responsibility. We can have faith in our Higher Power's ability to help them. And we can hope for the best.

Exercises

Exercise One

Make a List of the People Important in Your Daily Life. Now list the ways in which their problems affect you and the emotions they trigger (such as shame, fear, worry, anxiety, anger, or guilt).

In light of the ego/spirit split within yourself and others, which reactions are from your ego? How might your spirit respond differently? Identify attack and defend feelings and behaviors. What feelings and actions would best serve your true inner peace and happiness?

Exercise Two

Identify Tendencies Toward Worry. When, where, and about whom do you worry? What effect does it have? Does it ever solve a problem or prevent a harm from occurring? Identify the differences between worry and constructive problem solving. Now let go of worry in every area of your life. Visualize releasing it into the care of your Higher Power.

CHAPTER SIX

Other People's Successes

Comparison is the death of true self-contentment.

—John Powell

We may respond in many ways when other people win, succeed, or acquire something new. While we may want or pretend to feel happy for them, our true feelings are often resentment, anger, fear, envy, or depression. Our self-esteem may be damaged by comparisons we make of ourselves to other people. We may even respond in this way when those we love or feel close to achieve a goal or receive an unexpected boost.

Why do we react so negatively to such positive happenings? Because our ego feels threatened by every success outside of itself. When someone else gains something, our ego feels attacked, as if something has been taken away from it. Our ego constantly compares us to others, judging our gains and losses against theirs and filling us with fear and defensiveness.

We may fear losing our job or status at work when a co-worker receives a promotion. We may resent our neighbor for being able to afford a new car while we struggle on with our old clunker. We may believe our spouse or lover will leave us if he or she outgrows us financially, emotionally, intellectually, or socially. We may *know* these feelings are unfounded or irrational, but we may *feel* them all the same.

All of these reactions to other people's successes inflame our ego and destroy our peace and happiness. As Jerry Jampolsky writes, "There is no room for peace of mind or love in our hearts when the ego is telling us to value anger and hate." If we remember that we all have egos that view the world as finite, with only so much success and happiness to go around, we can understand these reactions. But we can also outgrow them. We can let go of our ego's mistaken beliefs, fears, and insecurities.

To understand our ego's reactions to others' good fortune and success, we first look to our childhood experiences to see where these reactions began. When we examine our early experiences, recognizing the traits of the ego that lives within us, we can see more clearly how our current feelings and behaviors resulted from them.

We are often taught from an early age to constantly compare ourselves to other people. Growing up in our families and schools we often found ourselves in competition with others for attention, money, material things, honors, prestige, and even love. This may be where we learned to fear other people's successes.

The Primal Rivalry

Our brothers and sisters were often our first competitors. We vied for the attention and affection of our parents, and discovered which ways we could gain their approval. We may have resented younger siblings as they robbed us of our parents' time and energy. We may even have plotted our revenge, treating our siblings with something less than "brotherly love."

If our parents compared us to one another, we may have developed deep resentments. We may have acted out those feelings by attacking our siblings overtly or in more subtle ways. We may have chosen to behave in the opposite manner when a brother or sister was praised for specific behavior. We may have gotten attention by simply being "naughty."

We may have been assigned a role in our family that made our good self-image rest on constant achievements. But we may also have been assigned a role that didn't allow for accomplishments and successes. Sometimes, our family role may be that of "the screw-up" or "the lazy one" or "the pretty but dumb one." These kinds of roles can make us feel as if certain types of achievements and successes simply aren't for us, and we may consequently resent others who do get them.

Our family of origin may have served as a blueprint for the way we saw and dealt with all the other groups in which we found ourselves later. We may have developed methods of getting attention or feeling successful that were destructive or self-defeating. We may still have old tapes playing in our minds saying things like, *Why can't you be like so-and-so?* We may react to everyone else's happiness and success by wailing, *What about me?*

Older brothers and sisters often feel that their parents allow their younger siblings to have more privileges or freedom at earlier ages than they were given. This is often because of the development of our parents' own abilities and experience in parenting. Sarah says that when she was sixteen, her parents tried to make up for the apparent discrepancies in what her younger sisters got to do by giving her her own bedroom and taking away her household chore responsibilities.

Sarah says, "The thing that seemed so unfair about it was that they took all the chores I had been doing by myself and split them between my three sisters. They each had to do *one-third* of what I'd been doing all along—*and they complained about it!* It just didn't seem fair, and it made me really mad when they had the nerve to complain."

It isn't only older children who feel these kinds of injustices and pressures. Younger children may feel a tremendous pressure to follow in the footsteps of their older siblings' accomplishments. Often, they have different talents or interests, which may not be as appreciated or accepted by the family. They may simply long for their individual identity to be recognized.

These kinds of early family experiences can have far-reaching effects in our adult lives. They teach our ego to fear and expect unfair treatment, and consequently develop jealousies and resentments toward others. Our spirits may never get the chance to show us how safe, secure, and happy we can feel no matter what others have or accomplish.

Other Parental Problems

There will never be perfect parents. Our parents may have unwittingly set us up in childhood for a lifetime of feeling undeserving of success or resentful of other people's. We may have learned to suppress our desire for respect and support for our accomplishments if we didn't get such nurturing from our parents. This suppressed need can come out later in the form of jealousy or resentment toward others.

When he was in high school, Brad was asked to speak at a baccalaureate ceremony. This was a very high honor, awarded to only one student in the entire school each year. Brad felt proud and pleased to have been chosen. He felt that all of his hard work in school was being respected and recognized.

"I was really nervous about it," Brad says. "But I worked hard on the speech and gave it my very best. I thought I did a pretty good job." After the ceremony, Brad's friends, teachers, and family congratulated him on his speech. "I felt really proud and wanted my parents to feel proud of me too. I really needed their approval and praise. But the first thing my mother said to me was, 'For a while there, we thought you were going to get long-winded—you know, like you do—but you ended up doing all right.'" His mother's comment robbed Brad of his feelings of success and pride. "It really took the wind out of my sails. I felt like a jerk. I couldn't stop worrying about what I had sounded like, what I had said. I felt awful."

Brad now says, "Maybe she didn't mean it, but what my mother did was take that important moment of success away from me. She just wouldn't let me enjoy it. I never felt comfortable with any kind of awards or accomplishments after that. I really felt like I didn't deserve them, like they'd be taken away from me if I let myself believe them or enjoy them too much."

When our parents fail to give us the respect and support we need for our accomplishments, we may develop this inability to enjoy our successes. We may also develop a corresponding resentment for other people's successes and their enjoyment of them. We may get caught up in our ego's fear that good feelings can and will always be taken away from us. We may not let ourselves experience our spirit's joy in our own and other people's accomplishments.

School

Even if we had no siblings or received remarkably evenhanded treatment from our parents, we quickly picked up the idea of comparison and competition in school. Unfortunately, we still haven't devised an educational system free of constant judging and comparing students against one another. Since school is such a big part of children's lives, we spent a great deal of time growing up in this competitive environment.

The joy of learning new things, of exploring all the fascinating aspects of math, science, language, and the arts may have been lost in the race for gold stars and big red A's. Developing skills and abilities may have become less important than class rankings. Accumulating knowledge may have taken a backseat to accumulating rewards.

Matthew says he dropped out of college in his freshman year because he was "so sick of the whole system of grades and all that nonsense." He explains, "When you're eighteen, you've spent your whole life in school, constantly being judged and compared to the other kids. I was smart and I always did well, but all that pressure took the fun—and the *interest*—out of learning for me."

After leaving college, Matthew traveled extensively, worked at all kinds of jobs, and "read voraciously." He says, "I'd always loved books. For as long as I could remember, books had been one of the greatest joys of my life. School had almost killed that joy for me. When I was working in a factory or driving a cab, I always had a book with me. I rediscovered my love of learning."

Matthew went back to college at age twenty-six and graduated with honors at thirty. "This time," he says, "I was there only for myself. I didn't care at all about grades or comparing myself to other students. I just *enjoyed* all the new ideas and knowledge I could absorb.

"The thing people don't seem to realize is that even when kids are getting straight A's, they don't necessarily come out of their school experience with healthy, high self-esteem. Sometimes it gives them an intensified sense of competition instead—a feeling that their self-image depends on all those silly rewards and symbols. They can never feel good about just *learning* or even just being themselves."

Sports and Games

In childhood we may also have learned to view sports and games as exercises in conquest, rather than skill and fun. We may have learned quickly that the only enjoyment in playing was in winning. It didn't take much to see that "the agony of defeat" was to be avoided at all costs. Many of us simply didn't take up sports if early on it seemed that we might not be star-player material.

Even our parents and teachers may have promoted the attitude that our opponents are always bad or un-deserving of our respect, simply because they were on the other side. Many of us weren't even taught to *act like* good sports whether or not we felt like it. This is unfortunate because such Acting As If can become habit. When it does, we can mature into the genuine feelings of happiness for others' successes and enjoying games for their own sake.

The reasons we have sports and games at all are often obscured by our overdeveloped sense of competition. Games of skill and strategy were developed very early in human history. They gave us opportunities to appre-ciate and enjoy other people's physical and mental

91

abilities. They gave us communal, recreational activities to enjoy together. They gave us diversions from our daily work.

But today, games and sports often seem fraught with the same stresses and pressures we need to get away from. We may treat them more like hard, unpleasant work than play. We may invest ourselves in them as if our self-image and emotional well-being depended on them. We may let our egos spoil the fun of every recreational activity we attempt.

Relearning how to enjoy sports and games can be done at any age. All we have to do is recognize our ego's fearful confusion about needing to win and feeling threatened when other people win. We can let go of these delusions and begin enjoying sports and games more than ever before. Our spirits can take over our attitudes and actions in this area of our lives, as in all others, and show us the joy of true play.

Our Self-Image

The most basic element of our ability to be happy for other people's happiness and success is our own self-image. If we are filled with inner peace and happiness, how can other people's successes possibly affect us negatively? If we are secure and confident in ourselves, how can other people's successes threaten us? If we know we are far more than our outer achievements and successes, why should we care about comparing them to anyone else's?

Our spirit doesn't care about any of these things. It is always completely peaceful and happy. It never compares us to others. It rejoices in *all* true happiness and success, regardless of who seems to have it. It knows it is not threatened by anything good happening to or for anyone else. It can't even conceive such a fearful thought.

If we live in our ego's shadow of fear and separateness, we can't help but feel threatened by the successes of others. But our spirit knows its oneness with all others, and therefore can only share the joy of their success, well-being, and true happiness. We can bring this sense of oneness with others into our conscious lives. We can allow ourselves to feel good for the successes of others.

Kevin discovered his ego's self-image when his wife became more successful than him financially. "I never thought I'd be one of those guys who felt threatened by having a wife who earned more money," he says. "But I realize now that when I thought that, I also believed there wasn't much chance of it actually happening to me. I was older than my wife, with more education and work experience, so it just seemed logical that I'd always make more money than she did."

When his wife wanted to quit her job to start her own business, Kevin was all for it. He says, "I figured I could easily support us on my income, and if she wanted to pursue this little hobby, I'd let her." But the "little hobby" quickly turned into a successful, money-making business.

"I'd never known she was such a businesswoman," Kevin says. "After the first year, her business was in the black, and after the second, she was bringing home twice as much money as I did. I was devastated. I treated her terribly. Instead of supporting her and being proud of her accomplishments, I complained all the time. I got mad because she wasn't at home as much as she used to be. I belittled her work and generally acted like a spoiled brat.

"To other people, I said I was happy for my wife's success. I said I loved the extra money, and made jokes about quitting my job and living off my rich wife. But inside, I was burning up. I hated myself. I felt as if the balance between us had shifted, and my whole self-image was shot. I didn't know who I was anymore. I looked around our house, saw things *her* money had bought everywhere, and felt like a failure."

Kevin's ego had convinced him that his self-image depended upon providing the monetary support for his family. When he was no longer needed to fulfill that function, he felt useless and fearful. He lost sight of his spirit's love and joy in his wife's success, and instead, allowed his ego to determine his self-image.

When we answer the question, *What am I?* with our spirit's certainty, trust, and invulnerability, we can accept other's successes with joy. When we know there is plenty of good to go around, we can be happy for others when they seem to get a little of it. When we are open to receiving our own successes, no one else's can detract from them in any way.

We can begin understanding that our ego's self-image is very different from our spirit's. We can accept our ego's fearfulness and defensiveness as the only way it can see the world. We can begin using the power we have to turn our minds from our ego's self-image to our spirit's. This power is the key to learning to accept—and even enjoy—other people's successes.

Envy and Jealousy

While the words are often used interchangeably, there is a subtle difference between *envy* and *jealousy*. *Webster's Dictionary* defines envy as: "discontent or ill will because of another's advantages, possessions . . .;

resentful dislike of another who has something desirable; desire for what another has." Envy is our ego saying, *I want what you have, and I hate you for having it.*

Jealousy is defined as suspicion, rivalry, possessiveness, and protectiveness of our possessions, relationships, and successes. Jealousy is our ego saying, *You can't have what I have, and I hate you for wanting, trying to get, or getting it.*

Jealousy and envy indicate that we have put specific conditions on our happiness. We believe that *If only I had that . . .* or *If only that other person didn't get that . . .* we'd be happy. Jealousy and envy are delusions that our happiness and well-being have something to do with whatever other people do or have.

Our ego is convinced that if another has something desirable, we are being deprived of it. So it wants whatever others have or achieve, and it carefully guards whatever it thinks we have. Our ego's viewpoint says that we are always in danger of losing what we have and never getting anything as good or better to replace it. Envy and jealousy are its defenses against these perceived threats.

Letting Go of Envy and Jealousy

Infinite abundance, generosity, and sharing are beyond the scope of our ego. Once we understand this, we can begin understanding many of our self-defeating attitudes and behaviors. We can begin turning away from our ego's defensive perceptions and opening up to our spirit's greater knowledge.

Sharing and enjoying the successes and happiness of others creates *more,* not less. Love extended to others grows and multiplies. Peace sent out into the world— even from just one person—expands and spreads throughout the universe. We can all gain by the true health, happiness, well-being, and success of others.

Conversely, fearful envy and jealousy only tighten our stranglehold on the portion of success we manage to grasp. The tighter we grip, the less we can really have. Our fear of losing out to others can only bring us unhappiness. Our joy for their successes can open us up to our own.

Justice

It is easy to feel happy for the success of someone who we believe deserves it. When we see long, hard work rewarded, it seems fitting. When we see abundance and happiness come to someone who has suffered, we deem it right and just. When someone who seems deprived in some areas gains something in another area, we call it balance or fairness.

But what about when someone seems to gain easily, without sacrifice or payment? What about people who seem to gain from activities that harm others—or at least don't seem to suffer for them? What about when good things happen to people who don't seem to deserve them?

Sometimes it may seem as if harmful behavior is actually rewarded. We may react angrily to the wealth of Wall Street manipulators or the re-election of corrupt politicians. We may feel outraged by the apparent success of others when we think they haven't earned it or haven't "paid" for some wrongdoing.

If we define "getting away with it" as escaping the legal system, then obviously many people "get away with" many crimes all the time. But if we define cosmic justice as the law of reaping as we sow, then there is no such thing as "getting away with" anything. Our inner peace, happiness, and well-being are always damaged by deceit and harm toward others or ourselves.

Alice's Story

When she was a teenager, Alice's best friend was killed in a hit-and-run car accident. "I was *so angry,*" Alice says. "My sense of justice was shattered. I couldn't believe a young life could just be taken away like that for no reason, and the person responsible could just walk away as if nothing had happened. I *hated* whoever was driving that car. I wanted the police to find the person *so badly.* I wanted a chance to scream at the person, to tell them what a great person they had killed, to see that driver suffer for it."

But her friend's mother took a different attitude than Alice's. "I couldn't believe the way she acted," Alice says. "She never wanted to hear about the efforts that were being made to find the driver of the car that killed her daughter. She said that finding the driver, trying the person in court, and punishing them in any way wouldn't bring her daughter back. She said whoever did it would have to live with it the rest of their lives and that it was between that person and God. She was a loving, peaceful woman, but at the time, I really thought she was crazy. I just couldn't share her viewpoint. I wanted blood for what had been done to my friend—and to *me.*"

The driver of the car that killed Alice's friend was never found. "It used to really bother me that out there somewhere, walking around, probably living a normal life, was the person who had killed her," she says. "I used to be afraid that it was someone I knew, someone I met after it happened, someone I worked with or lived

97

next door to. I used to walk around all the time, looking at strangers and thinking, 'It could be *you.*'"

Alice says that now, nearly twenty years after it happened, she feels more as her friend's mother did then. "All the anger only hurt myself," she says. "Nothing could have undone what happened. I don't know what became of the person who did it, but I do know that what I wanted to do to that person was no better than what he or she did to my friend, and wouldn't have helped anything.

"Maybe the person did go on and live a happy life, but I doubt it. I think something happens inside us when we do something harmful to another person, and sooner or later we have to deal with that. It's not even a guilty conscience, necessarily, but more like a *separating* from ourselves—from the good part that's in each and every one of us. In order to have any real peace or happiness, we have to mend that separation by doing some good, making some kind of amends. So maybe whoever drove that car eventually did something good in the world. But if not, it's not my problem. It's God's."

Forgiveness

Alice learned to forgive the person whose action caused her friend's death. This kind of forgiveness is a big part of learning to let go of our negative reactions to other people's successes. As long as we believe that someone owes a debt or deserves a punishment, we can never feel happy for his or her successes, achievements, or happiness.

Our judgments may seem quite reasonable and justified in many instances. We don't have to abandon our ideas of right and wrong in order to forgive. We simply have to accept the reality of what is and move forward from there. We have to let go of harboring feelings of revenge or punishment. They can never have positive effects on ourselves or anyone else.

When we see something good happening to someone we judge as undeserving, we can remember that we just don't know everything about that person, or have the true perspective to judge him or her. We can also remember that what appears to us to be success and happiness isn't always so. We can let go of our self-defeating anger and turn our attention to more positive attitudes and actions.

Who Deserves It More?

Sometimes people compete for a job, promotion, or prize of some kind, and we don't think the right person wins. Sometimes more factors enter into the choice than we think legitimately should. *Sometimes life just isn't fair.* Whenever this happens, we can always choose how we will respond.

Our ego wants a nice, clear, "eye for an eye" kind of justice. It can't accept the possibility of things happening in the world outside of its awareness. It can't see the larger scheme of things or trust in anything outside itself. It wants visible proof of evenhanded rewards and punishments. Our spirit simply doesn't care about such things. While our ego reacts with anger and defensiveness, our spirit feels just fine. It knows we are always okay, no matter what happens. It accepts *all* the "wins" and "losses" of life as they come.

Disappointment is natural when we don't get something we want. But when we turn our disappointment against someone else because they got what we wanted or got something we didn't think they deserved, we are only exercising our ego's defensiveness. There is plenty of good in life to go around. We just have to clear out all our anger and resentment toward others in order to see it.

Scarcity

Our beliefs in the scarcity of achievements and good feelings can cripple our ability to enjoy the successes of others. If we believe there is only so much success possible—if someone must always win and someone must always lose—then it can be very hard to feel good about other people winning. We feel the crunch of limited resources whenever we see another walk away with a prize. We let our ego convince us that there's nothing left over for us.

Here again, we can understand our ego's fearfulness and let it go. We can turn to our spirit's view, which sees success and happiness as unlimited for us all. We can learn to see everyone's success as contributing positively to everyone else's. Other people's success can often be the best thing for all of us.

Sometimes our scarcity beliefs can stop us from accepting our own successes. We may feel guilty, as if we're taking something away from others by succeeding. We may have learned to view success as wrong when our parents expressed resentment for others' successes.

If we allow our egos to convince us that success is a limited resource, we will always feel guilty for having any, and resentful of others who have it. But if we let our spirits show us the infinite abundance of success and happiness available to us all, we can never feel deprived or ashamed for our achievements. Instead, we can accept and enjoy our own success, and therefore be able to accept and enjoy other people's as well.

In Competition with Ourselves

William George Jordan wrote, "The true competition is the competition of the individual with himself, his present seeking to excel his past. This means real growth from within." If we always require someone to "beat" in order to feel successful, we may never truly feel satisfied. There is always another challenger to face, and they must all be seen as enemies. Where is the joy in this? When we concentrate on learning, growing, and being our own true best selves, we can enjoy the successes of others as much as our own. We can even appreciate the skill and accomplishments of our competitors.

The respect Olympic athletes often display for one another is a good example of this kind of joy. They know their opponents have trained and worked as long and as hard as they have. They admire each other's skill and accomplishments. They enjoy each other's performances perhaps more than spectators do, because they know exactly what it feels like to do what they're doing and how difficult it really is.

It can feel good to see someone else succeed if we stop letting our ego take everyone else's accomplishments as a personal attack. When we stop competing against other people and learn instead to compete against our own past performances, we can discover the inherent joy of continual self-improvement. Then we can allow our spirits to teach us to share others' successes with love and happiness.

Exercises

Exercise One

Examining Childhood Experiences. What kinds of relationships did you have with your brothers and sisters

101

(or other peers living in your home)? Did you feel competitive or resentful toward them? How were your feelings dealt with in your family? Think about your early school experiences. Did you feel competitive toward the other students? Were these feelings encouraged or discouraged? How do these early experiences affect your attitudes and behaviors now? Can you see any similarity between the way you felt and reacted to others now and then?

Exercise Two

Clearing Up and Clearing Out Scarcity Beliefs. Examine your beliefs about the availability of success and happiness for everyone. Do you think there is only a small amount to go around?

Visualize a world of infinite possibilities of success and happiness for all. Imagine that *everyone* has totally equal opportunities for accomplishing their goals and achieving their dreams. Remember that no one is ever hurt or deprived in any way by anyone else's successes. Everyone lives in harmony and joy for each other's achievements. Imagine how much all these accomplishments and successes would contribute to the whole of humanity.

Exercise Three

Competition. Try watching a competition (athletic, academic, or whatever interests you) where you have no knowledge of or connection to any of the opponents. In other words, you really don't care who wins. Try to just enjoy the game for its own sake. Watch things like individual skills, team efforts, or the rules and design of the game itself. If you're watching sports on television, try turning off the sound to eliminate the broadcaster's comments. Just be an impartial observer. Discover all the elements of the game other than winning and losing.

CHAPTER SEVEN

Work

You are not what you do; you are how you do it.

—Hugh Prather

We all work. Whether we spend our days at home, in an office, factory, restaurant, school, or store; at a construction site or on the road; up in the sky or down in a mine, we *all* work. Whether it's cooking, typing, caring for our elderly parents or raising children; selling or buying; designing, building, or tearing down; cleaning, serving, or managing, it's all work. The only differences are in *where* we do it and *how* we do it.

Where we work matters little; *how* we work matters a lot. How we work involves a combination of our beliefs, feelings, attitudes, and behaviors. It's the way we see ourselves, our job, and the people we work with. It's an expression of our basic approach toward life. It can keep us stuck in misery and pain, or fill us with joy and love. If it's not helping us discover happiness, it can always be changed.

One of the ways in which our approach to work can impede our growth and happiness is by entangling our work with our self-image or identity. We may choose our jobs based on the effect we think they will have on other people's impressions of us. Or we may feel angry, ashamed, or resentful because we feel our work doesn't reflect our true abilities and talents. All of this is caused by our ego's insistence that we *are* what we *do*.

"What do you do?"

Imagine meeting someone for the first time, talking with the person and getting to know him or her, *without asking what he or she does for a living*. We are so used to getting right to the question, "What do you do?" that this may seem ridiculous. We may wonder how we can get to know people without knowing what they do for a living. But we may really be *judging* them and assuming all kinds of things about their intelligence, attitudes, and general worth based on their job.

These are really the only functions that can be served by learning what others do for a living immediately upon meeting them. We form an opinion of them based on their job and its status or influence. We determine if they can do anything to further our own ambitions. We judge their value to us, others, and society by what they do for a living.

In many foreign countries it is considered unpardonably rude to ask people we don't know well what kind of work they do. It would be like asking a new acquaintance how much money he or she makes. But Americans consider a person's job to be important information *before* we decide how to treat the person or whether to bother getting to know him or her better. Our culture obsessively defines people as their work.

"Just a housewife."

While her children were small, Amanda stayed at home to raise them. She considered this to be important work, and devoted herself to her children's care, education, and emotional well-being. She was very talented at this and loved doing it. But Amanda always felt that others looked down on her for choosing to spend her time and talents in this way.

"I'd be at a party with my husband," she says, "and people would come up to me, introduce themselves, tell me what they did for a living, and then ask me what I did. When I said I was at home with two preschoolers, they'd say something like, 'Oh, really?' and promptly move on to talk to someone else. It was like they instantly assumed I couldn't possibly have anything interesting to say or be able to carry on an intelligent conversation with another adult about anything other than diaper rash!"

Amanda continues, "These people didn't know me at all, but they thought they did, just by knowing what kind of work I was doing at that time in my life. It really made me angry, and if I'm honest, a little ashamed of myself. They made me feel like maybe what I was doing *wasn't* so important after all, or maybe I just *couldn't* do anything else. I was filled with self-doubt after those incidents, and my self-esteem felt battered."

Respect

We not only believe that people are what they do, but we also tend to equate the value of a job with its income. When we are unemployed, homemaking, or working at low-paying jobs, we often feel less *valuable* than others. Even if we enjoy and take pride in our work, as Amanda did, our ego may feel threatened by the lack of respect we get from other people for doing it.

This disrespect can trigger our ego's defensiveness and create anger, embarrassment, resentment, sadness, and self-doubt. It can be so demoralizing that we actually quit a job we feel others disrespect, or we may stop caring about doing it well. We might adopt a negative, bored, cynical attitude toward our work as a defense against what we feel are other people's attacks on our self-respect. Our ego says, *I don't really care about this job, so don't identify me with this.*

There is a difference between wanting to *impress* people with what we do and wanting to be *respected* for it. When we impress other people, they make a fuss over us, and perhaps see us in an inflated, unrealistic way. When we are respected, people accept us as we are and don't make assumptions about us based on our work or anything else.

Impression comes from our ego, respect comes from our spirit. I believe respect is a basic human right. We have a right to feel a need and desire for it. We have a right to expect it from everyone in our lives. We also have a responsibility to extend it to others. Respect is one of the most valuable gifts we can share with each other.

Are We What We Do?

If we define ourselves and others by the work we do, then every crisis, every problem, every little up and down of our job takes on the enormous significance of supporting our ego's self-image. We can't have a minor setback at work without feeling as if our world is ending. We can't separate our problems at work from our self-esteem. We can't feel comfortable and content unless our work life is going along perfectly.

If we allow our ego to define us as our work and its rewards, we're at the mercy of many factors outside of our control. We may end up devaluing the other areas of our lives and running ourselves ragged trying to accomplish the impossible. We may neglect our real talents, abilities, potential achievements, relationships, and other possible sources of joy and healthy self-esteem.

Patricia says, "I used to feel my work was what made me who I was. I did everything that was asked of me, and more. I took over all of my boss' responsibilities when she suddenly quit, and I worked nonstop, day and night, for six months. I finally collapsed and went on a week-long drinking binge, ending up in the hospital. I had neglected every area of my life except work, and I had to start all over again figuring out what those other areas were and what I needed to do about them.

"I love my current job," Patricia says, "and I feel it's what I'm supposed to be doing right now. But it's not my whole life or self; it's only one part of my purpose on this earth. Now I know that I'm a lot more than what I do."

When we remember that we are indeed much more than what we do for a living, we can rediscover our true identity as spiritual beings. We can keep our work in perspective, as only one part of a full life. We can give the attention necessary to all the important areas of our lives, while maintaining our true self-image and identity.

A Good Job

What do we look for in a job? Do we just go out and try to get whatever kind of work we can? Do we look for the highest pay? The most convenient hours? The most interesting work? The least difficult duties? Friendly co-workers? Do we want our job to provide prestige? Opportunities for a better future? A chance to use our own particular skills and talents? What is a "good job" to us?

William George Jordan wrote, "No matter how humble the calling of the individual, how uninteresting and dull the round of his duties, he should do his best. He should dignify what he is doing by the mind he puts into it." If we let go of our ego's self-image as nothing more than what we do for a living, we can begin concentrating on *how* we do it. Faith, hope, love, and joy can be brought to any honest work. When we turn our minds to our spirit's viewpoint, we can elevate our work to its level.

"What do you expect from this job?"
Many of us don't think about what we expect from our work. We may think of work as nothing more than an unpleasant necessity. We may hurry up the corporate ladder without ever asking ourselves, *Why?* We may follow in the patterns of our parents and other role models without realizing there could be another way of looking at work.

Our expectations are powerful elements of our achievements. If we expect too much from our work, we are likely to feel disappointed. If we expect too little, we'll probably feel dissatisfied, resentful, and angry. We may sabotage our chances for success and happiness in our work simply by harboring unrealistic expectations.

What *can* we expect from our work? Can everyone expect the same things from their work, no matter what they do? Of course not. We work at various kinds of jobs at various times in our lives. They serve different purposes and can be expected to fill different needs. When we are just starting out in our work life, we often take jobs simply to gain experience or to make some money for school or to help out our family. We learn a great deal from these early experiences, and often carry these attitudes and habits into the rest of our work lives. Sometimes we learn negative attitudes or expectations from unpleasant experiences early in our work lives. Sometimes we develop good working habits and realistic expectations.

At other times in our work life, we take jobs for other reasons. We may choose a job because of its proximity to our home, school, or our children's school. We may look for flexible hours, specific benefits, or a certain kind of experience to help us get an even better job later on. We may be attracted to certain types of work because they make use of specific abilities we have. There is nothing wrong with any of these reasons to choose a job, and we are often satisfied with these choices.

But when our expectations are unrealistic or negative, we can set ourselves up for unhappiness. Often, we think of work as merely a necessary burden to pay for the things we really want. We endure it only to get to our "real life" after working hours. While our job may not be the main focus or most fulfilling area of our lives, we can expect more from it than forty hours of misery each week, punctuated by periods of frantic recreation or material consumption to make up for it.

Work doesn't have to be unpleasant drudgery that feels good only on payday. When we find ways to put ourselves into our work, we can discover the many purposes work can serve to enrich and enhance our lives. It can bring us into contact with other people. It can help us discover and develop our talents and abilities. It can provide us with the joy of learning new things and developing skills. It can bring us the satisfaction of trying something difficult and meeting the challenge.

If we are not finding these joys in our work, maybe we need to find another job or kind of work. Or maybe we need to examine our own attitudes and expectations. It's hard to find joy in something we truly believe to be joyless. But if we open our minds to our spirit's joyful viewpoint, we just might be surprised to find opportunities for learning, growing, and enjoyment right under our noses.

Blooming Where We Are Planted

Tina tells us, "At one point in my work life, I found myself in a job I felt was boring, frustrating, and leading nowhere. But I needed to keep it while continuing my education and being available to my children after school hours. At work, I constantly thought about the day, somewhere off in the future, when I'd be able to quit and do something else. Then one day during this time, I spotted a poster that said, 'Bloom where you are planted.' I thought this was a good, uplifting sentiment and one I needed to remember as I plodded along through this period in my work life.

"I mentioned the quote to a co-worker who was complaining, as usual, about her boredom and frustration with her dead-end job. But rather than finding it inspiring, as I had, she got mad at me. She said it was a depressing, condescending statement to encourage people not to try to better themselves. I said I didn't see it that way, and I couldn't help wondering what all her constant complaining was doing to better herself."

At various times in our lives, we may find ourselves, like Tina, in jobs we don't like very much. If we have examined the situation and determined that we need to remain at this job at least for a while, we can then proceed to find ways in which the job can make use of our talents and abilities, teach us something, and enable us to find pride and joy in the work—to "bloom where we are planted."

It may seem easier to just complain about the situation, like Tina's co-worker, than try to make something better out of it. It may even seem *impossible* to find anything good about the situation. If this is really true, we probably should re-examine our choice to stay in the job. But our blocks to enjoying and growing through some part of the job may merely be ego games.

There is a difference between pointless complaining and constructive problem solving. Complaining has no intention or direction toward solving anything. It's just "blowing off steam," venting frustration, looking for company in misery. It's our ego's way of keeping us stuck in unhappiness. It's contagious and demoralizing.

Constructive problem solving is trying to use our abilities, talents, and cooperation to bring about positive change. It isn't always met with understanding and joy by co-workers or even bosses, who may prefer to stay with the status quo no matter what, in hopes of keeping their jobs or reputations as good, trouble-free workers. But when problem solving is done in a peaceful, positive manner, it is the only way for any organization to stay alive and growing.

If we continue just complaining and waiting for something better to come along, we may not recognize it when it does. Or we may not be prepared to take advantage of it. For example, if we show only disinterest and frustration with our current job, giving only the minimum of effort needed to do it, we won't be in a very good position to be promoted or transferred. Negative attitudes and behaviors also tend to become habitual. We may create our own dead ends by refusing to look for anything positive in our work, or not believing positive change is possible.

We also grow more and more angry, bored, and sour by allowing our egos to sink into these feelings. Things won't ever get better by magic. We have to make the effort, take the time, and try to find the best point of view to make things better for ourselves. We can either quit the job or quit complaining. We can try to effect positive change, in a cooperative manner, or accept things as they are. We can choose to find our happiness regardless of the job circumstances in which we find ourselves.

What Is My Mission?

We can find something positive to focus on in our work by identifying our mission. Sometimes, our only reason for working at a job is to support our family or put our children through school. These can be very fulfilling goals. If we concentrate on helping our family in this way, we can see the value and importance in what we're doing.

We can also examine the contribution our work makes to the world. This can sometimes be difficult because of the blocks our egos have created in our minds. But there is inherent value in every kind of honest work. Cooking or serving food is a great and necessary service to hungry human beings. Doing it with a manner of calm friendliness and joy is an added blessing. Washing floors, cars, windows, or dishes can contribute to the health and comfort of many. Working on an assembly line, making our small part of some larger product, provides a service to the other workers as well as the consumer of a safe, functional product.

In his book, *When All You've Ever Wanted Isn't Enough,* Rabbi Harold Kushner writes, "Some jobs can afford to be done poorly and no one will be hurt, but none of us can afford the internal spiritual cost of being sloppy in our work." If we don't find a way to give our work something of ourselves, to discover the positive contribution we are making in it, we won't be able to derive any satisfaction or joy from it. When we focus our attention on the positive effects or aspects of our work, we can begin releasing our ego's negative feelings about other aspects we may not enjoy.

Right Livelihood
There are certain elements of our work that make it more joyful and fulfilling for us. We need to examine these elements in order to choose the best work for us. Sometimes we feel we need to take whatever work we can get, but, even then, we do have certain criteria for the kinds of work we are willing to do. For example, we won't do anything illegal, or we won't work certain hours or too far from home.

We may feel many of these criteria are givens, that they go without saying. But we really need to examine all of them to learn about ourselves and the kinds of work we'd most like to do. When we don't examine them, we may find ourselves unhappy with our work and not understanding the reasons.

"Right Livelihood" is the term the Buddha used to describe one of the eight elements of a well-lived life. It means work that harms no one in any way; that makes use of our abilities and talents; that helps other people and the world in some way, however small. It means useful, positive, and meaningful work.

Throughout this book, we have examined our beliefs, attitudes, and behaviors *pragmatically*. We can apply this same method to examining our work. We can ask ourselves first, *Is it harmless?* and then, *Is it helpful?* Right livelihood gives meaning to our daily activities and provides us with at least one outlet for our abilities, talents, and skills. It helps us find peace of mind, happiness, and joy.

How do we determine whether our work fulfills these requirements? One of the first places to look is within our own feelings. If we are constantly bored, angry, frustrated, or fearful about our work, we must ask ourselves, *Why?* If the work harms others in some way, this harms us on a deep spiritual level. We can never feel good about work that is harmful. If our work seems meaningless or unnecessary, how can we find joy or pride in it?

We can examine these feelings to find our true joy and love, and follow these feelings to the work we should be doing. But we can also uncover false pride and ego games that stand in our way. Scrubbing floors may not be our idea of a good job, but it does not harm anyone. If we feel sad, angry, or embarrassed to do this kind of work, that may be a pride issue—a problem for our ego, not our spirit.

When we have examined the reasons for our discontent, we can begin analyzing how we need to change our attitudes and behaviors, and what elements we need to look for in a job. Some of these are universal, and some will be very particular for us.

Some universal elements of a good job are: that it's legal; that it doesn't harm anyone, including ourselves; and that it makes some kind of contribution to others. Some more specific, individual elements might include

116

a certain level of income, benefits we need for ourselves or our family, opportunities for learning and progressing in our career, and using our specific talents and abilities.

Right livelihood is a matter of our individual circumstances and abilities. We find it when we let go of all those ego games and delusions that keep us stuck in unrealistic expectations or negative attitudes and beliefs. When we let our spirits guide us, right livelihood becomes an easy choice.

What Do I Love?

When we've let go of our ego's ideas about the misery of work, we can begin looking for the work we love and do best. Often, we know early in our lives what kind of work we'll do well and enjoy most, but we get sidetracked or discouraged from pursuing it. One woman showed such an artistic talent early in her life that her sixth-grade teacher gave her a wooden paintbox and palette to encourage her. After many years of working in a bank, this woman finally enrolled in art school and began a career as an illustrator.

When we examine our early experiences to discover the things we loved doing, we may find clues to the kinds of work we can enjoy now. If we examine the job market first to see what's available, without asking ourselves what we really want to do, we may end up miserable in a job we don't like and can't care about.

When we explore all the possibilities available to us in terms of work, we *start* by examining what we love. Therein lies the key to our right livelihood. We can discover ways to direct our joys into successful and fulfilling work, whether we enjoy sewing, cooking, numbers, books, children, sports, computers, drawing, negotiating, teaching, listening, building, cleaning, decorating, animals, gardening, or driving.

We can let what we love and our spirits lead us to our right livelihood. Don't look for perfection—you'll never find it. Look for work that harms no one, including yourself, work that you can feel good about, that makes some kind of positive contribution, however small, to people and the world. Look for work that makes use of your talents and abilities, and helps you to grow.

Discovering the Possibilities

Gary tells us that drugs dictated his every action when he was actively addicted to them. "I didn't have to figure out what I was going to do with my time," he says. "Drugs were always telling me, *Get up, go to the cabinet, get a glass, pour a drink, sit down and drink it, take a shower, smoke a joint . . .* and on and on like that—all day, every day. Drugs told me what to do with *all* of my time."

After getting sober and beginning a recovery program, Gary felt a lot of "I oughta's." He says, "I kept thinking, *I oughta be happy because I'm not dead; I oughta just shut up and be satisfied that I have a job at all, even though I hate it. I oughta be glad because I'm alive, clean, and sober.* But being alive was just like it used to be. It was a little different, but it took me a long time to understand what that difference was."

Gary says he was a full year into his recovery before he began realizing that he could choose how to spend his time. He says, "It took me a long time to get a new outlook on what I could do. For a long while, everything had seemed *impossible* to me. I even had a lot of people encouraging me to do things, to make a job or career change, but I thought, *I can't do that—that's something* normal *people do.* But gradually I realized that my time was my own to use any way I wanted to, and I was still wasting it—and I didn't have to do that. I quit my job and got into a training program to counsel adolescent drug addicts. I felt that was something I knew a lot about and that I could really help those kids."

Now, Gary says, "I've come to feel like work is so much more than just a paycheck. I'm finding I can invest myself in my work. I'm starting to stretch my outlook on what work is, to believe that it can be a part of who I am, and enhance who I am, and help me to grow and be a better person. I'm beginning to feel that if my work doesn't do that for me, then I do not want to do that work."

Realizing that the choice is ours about how we spend the working portion of our lives can be a tremendous turning point. We can begin looking at ourselves and our work very differently. We can begin examining all the possibilities we never knew existed. We can discover all the contributions we can make to other people and the world, and all the learning and growth that are available to us through our work. The world needs our contributions, and we need to make them.

Ethics in the Workplace

No one needs a job that hurts them spiritually. Going against our own inner sense of right and wrong, our basic moral understanding, day after day, corrodes our spiritual health, our inner peace and happiness. There's just no getting away from it. As Paul Pearsall writes, "It is not possible to separate our personal values from our daily work. . . . When we work, our spirit is listening."

Jake took evening classes while working full time in the construction business. He hoped to one day own a construction firm. In a class, Jake heard a man speak about his small advertising company. "The guy was *very* successful," Jake says. "I really wanted to learn all I could from him and his experiences. But one of the first things he said really threw me off. He said that he absolutely refused to work on any ad campaigns for cigarettes, alcohol, or politics. One of the other students said, 'Sure, you can afford to do that now that you're so successful.' But he smiled and said, 'I've been doing it since the day I started in this business. I can't afford *not* to.' I had never thought about ethics in business that way before. I'd seen a lot of stuff I considered unethical and just thought they were necessary business practices, things you *had* to do to get ahead. But I started thinking differently after taking that class."

We *can* maintain our ethics within our work situations and relationships, even if we don't own our own company. Being true to our inner sense of right and wrong doesn't mean we have to go around "blowing the whistle" on every injustice or irregularity we see. Our ego is very quick to judge others and point the finger of blame. But all we are really responsible for is our own behavior. If we concentrate on thinking things through carefully, rather than *reacting,* we can begin making sensible choices about what we are and aren't willing to do in our work.

Allison's Ethical Dilemma

Allison worked for an insurance company, making changes to existing policies. When an order came through to replace a low-cost, high coverage policy for an elderly client with a more expensive one offering less coverage, she questioned it. "My boss said that the order came from one of our best salesmen," she says. "He had been one of the company's top-selling employees for years, and we couldn't question his practices. I said I felt like I was cheating an old man out of money, and I felt we shouldn't process the order without calling the client to make sure he understood what he was buying. My boss took the case away from me and did it herself. The guy was sold something he didn't need and couldn't afford, but *I* didn't do it."

Sometimes this is all we can do when we see an injustice like the one Allison describes. She says she has always liked her job and tries to be a good worker. When she saw something that felt wrong to her, she brought it to her boss's attention—not in an angry or judgmental way, but as a truly concerned employee. She wasn't able to change company policy or prevent the harm from being done, but she calmly expressed her discomfort with it. And, who knows? Maybe her boss discussed it with the salesman or others in authority to avoid future occurrences. When we act from the calm, peaceful viewpoint of our spirit, we aren't always aware of the seeds we plant for positive change.

Sometimes a voice is needed to express what many of us are thinking. If we're all too afraid to say anything about a policy or action that seems harmful or unethical, it will never be changed. Sometimes asking a question about it can be an effective way to open up the subject and help create the possibility for positive change. A question is less threatening than a statement that *judges* the policy or action and *demands* change.

If you are in a position to make or change policy for the better, do so—in as calm and loving a manner as you can. If you are in a position of carrying out the policies made by others, you will have to make careful, calm decisions about what you will and will not do, and where you are willing to work. In either case, we can remember that anger, blame, and recriminations are of the ego, while positive, constructive change is of the spirit.

Good, Honest Work

We can also remember that being hurt spiritually is not the same as offending our ego. As long as we equate our self-image with our work, we can feel angry, embarrassed, or sad if our job isn't impressive enough in our eyes, or if we think others look down on it. We may confuse this ego-reaction with needing to leave a job because it truly harms us in some way.

We can live with work that offends our ego, if we recognize our ego's judgments and reactions. We can find joy in a job well done, bills paid, our family fed. We can discover ways to put our spirits into our work, whatever kind of work it may be. But we can't escape the inevitable damage to our inner peace if we leave our values and ethics behind when we go to work.

Unemployment

At some point in our working lives, most of us find ourselves unemployed. We're either looking for work and not finding it right away, or we might have a job and lose it for any number of reasons. Or perhaps we try a business venture that fails. Whatever the circumstances, unemployment can affect our feelings about work, ourselves, and other people.

If we define ourselves as our work, unemployment can be a devastating blow to our self-image. But it can also be exactly what we need to discover that we are far more than our work, or to find other talents, abilities, and ways we can contribute to the world and to grow within ourselves.

Unemployment can trigger our ego's defensiveness and create an attitude of resentment, anger, and blame. Our ego can also turn its anger against ourselves, in the form of depression, self-pity, and hopelessness. But our spirit waits quietly beneath the rantings and ravings of our ego, and knows our inner peace and happiness don't depend on any particular employment situation. Our spirit can fill us with hope, faith, acceptance, and fresh, new ideas for our future. It can heal our fearfulness and direct us to another, more positive point of view.

William George Jordan wrote, "Failure is often the turning point, the circumstance that swings us to higher levels." If we turn from our ego's viewpoint of unemployment as "failure," we can discover successes we may never have imagined before. We can follow our spirit's guidance toward better things to come.

Acceptance

Most of us need to work in order to earn a living. *All* of us work, in one way or another. Like all the other areas of our lives, work will provide us with some difficulties, setbacks, and changes to face. These are not necessarily bad things to be feared and avoided. They are a normal part of adult life.

Work is an area of life that can offer us great opportunities to learn, grow, and contribute our gifts to other people and the world. When we accept the ups and downs with hope, faith, and an open mind, they can all teach us something valuable. When we know we are far more than just our job or title, we can let go of our ego's fears and defensiveness.

Problems, disagreements, and differences of opinion don't have to mean the end of a job for us. We can learn to express ourselves calmly, guided by our spirit. We can learn to compromise, listen to others' viewpoints, and accept the realities of dealing with other people at work. We can learn to choose our battles carefully and take a stand when necessary. We can view our work through the eyes of our spirit and discover its place in our peaceful, happy lives.

Exercises

Exercise One

Am I What I Do? Examine the Relationship Between Your Work and Your Self-Image. How do you see yourself in terms of your work? Proud? Angry? Resentful? How would your self-image change if you changed jobs? Have you neglected any areas of your life in order to focus your time and energy on your work? How can you change your self-image to include all the aspects of your self and your life?

Exercise Two

What's a Good Job? Examine Your Beliefs About the Requirements for a Good Job. What elements do you believe are necessary in general? What specifics are necessary for you? Does your current work fulfill these requirements? If not, are you working toward another position that will? What are your expectations of your job? Are they realistic?

Exercise Three

Right Livelihood. Begin your search for right livelihood by asking yourself, *What do I love?* Examine your early experiences to see if you can discover what kind of work you'd like to do now. What were your favorite subjects in school? What did you like about them? Did you have any favorite hobbies or interests? How might they be brought into your work life? For a moment, just forget about the question of income, and think about your image of the ideal work for you—if you didn't have to work for money, what would you like to do? Why? What elements of this fantasy can you incorporate into your real work life?

CHAPTER EIGHT

Money

There is nothing in the world so demoralizing as money.

—Sophocles

The Greek dramatist, Sophocles, made this observation more than 2,400 years ago. It seems just as true today. No matter how much or how little we have, money can be an important and difficult issue for us all.

We may see money as our salvation from all the miseries of life or merely as a necessary evil. We may feel guilty for having it or angry for not having it. We may consider it a necessary condition for our happiness or a powerful temptation, distracting us from our "higher" purposes. What we see as the role of money in our lives may be causing us problems in one way or another.

What Is Money?

Most of us learned early in life that "money doesn't grow on trees." But we may never have pondered the powerful, underlying truth of this statement. *Money does not occur naturally in the universe.* It's a human invention, originally intended to ease trade. If there were no such thing as money, there would still be all the natural resources and human intelligence and skill to design

127

and make all the things in the world today. In fact, there would probably be *more* skilled, educated people if they didn't have to find a way to pay for their education, and more useful products that are now impossible to sell or manufacture for strictly financial reasons.

Money was originally designed to simplify trade—it was easier than having to carry around sheep to trade for pigs, or eggs to trade for grain. I don't have to tell you what a complicated mess our modern-day systems of economy have become. But what we often forget is that money, in itself, has no power. We associate money with certain feelings, beliefs, and attitudes, and then think that the money itself creates those feelings and attitudes.

"Money can burn you."

People often talk about money as if it's alive, as if it can do things to us. Stan says, "Money is like fire: Fire can be the best thing that ever happened, but it can also burn you. It can devastate you, consume you, and take everything else that you've got. Money can do all of those things and maybe even more, maybe even *worse,* because it can be more subtle."

Money doesn't really do any of those things—it can't actually *do* anything. *We* are responsible for our own beliefs, feelings, attitudes, and doing something about our problems with money. Blaming money itself is no different than blaming other people for our problems, feelings, behaviors, or lives. When we begin understanding our own roles and responsibilities regarding money, we can let go of our ego's desire to blame money for the difficulties we have with it.

"I would rather there were no money," Stan continues, "but I'm afraid that because of man's nature, if it weren't money it would just be something else." The part of "man's nature" Stan is talking about is our ego. Our ego gets wrapped up in money very easily because it is one of those outer conditions that we can focus on to avoid our true, inner selves. It's an easy target for our ego's blaming, defensive viewpoint. We can use it as an excuse for many negative, self-defeating attitudes and behaviors.

Taking Responsibility for Our Attitudes

Money is only demoralizing if *we* make it that way, if we respond to the idea of money in that way. We may remain ignorant of basic information about money, and then become angry when we get a bill we don't understand or overdraw our account at the bank. We may go around saying we *hate* money, and at the same time, wonder why we don't have more of it. Or we may accumulate more and more money and all the things it can buy, and wonder why we're still not happy.

Stan says he still doesn't like money, even now that he has to deal with more than he ever had to before. But he says he's "happy to be learning more about it." When we learn more about money, we can begin using it in a rational, relaxed way, letting go of our ego's grasp on it. We can learn to stop blaming money for its role in our lives and begin taking responsibility for our own feelings, attitudes, and finances.

Author Hugh Prather writes, "The world's two attitudes about money are that it is wonderful and it is evil. These are . . . only different sides of the same misplaced emphasis." Whether we worship money or hate it, we are giving it our personal power and responsibility. *We* choose the role money plays in our lives. We choose our own beliefs, attitudes, and actions toward money.

And we can choose to look at money in a new way. But first we have to examine our current beliefs and attitudes about money.

Worshipping Money

One of the ways in which we give money our power and responsibility is by worshipping it. We may believe we need it to be happy. We may believe it can buy us love, freedom, success, and joy. Getting more and more of it may become the central focus of our lives. But we can never get enough of it because it is our ego that wants it, and our ego's appetite is insatiable.

If we accept this viewpoint, then most of us must resign ourselves to unhappiness, because most of us are *not* wealthy. We can then either spend all our time and energy trying to get wealthy, or resenting others who we think are wealthier than we are. We may feel deprived, angry, sad, and envious of those who we think have more than we do. Or, if we are wealthy, we may wonder why we still aren't truly happy, worry about losing our money, or feel jealous and fearful of others who we think want what we have.

Our Self-Image

We may allow our ego to convince us that we need money—or a great deal of money—to feel good about ourselves. We may think other people will accept, respect, or like us better if we have more money. We may expect money to solve all our problems and difficulties, and make up for all of our shortcomings.

Money can become a substitute for working through our feelings, beliefs, and attitudes. It may be used as an excuse for ignoring other important areas of our life. We may believe that if we can only get enough money,

none of the other stuff will matter. We may even convince ourselves that having more money will make us
better people.

Our Personal Values

If we are using money, or the lack of it, as an excuse
for unhappiness and self-defeating behavior, we may
also begin ignoring our own values and ethics. We may
get caught on a downward spiral of excusing any kind
of illegal or unethical behavior that results in a monetary
gain for us. We may try to ignore the inner pain caused
by this negative behavior, using more and more money
to anesthetize ourselves with outer luxuries.

As I discussed in the chapter on work, we cannot
escape the inner pain of going against our own personal
values. One way or another, this pain will find us. Our
inner peace and happiness come first, at the center of
our personal energy and lives. Our self-image cannot
rest on our bank accounts or material possessions. If
we try to live this way, we set ourselves up for the
agony of struggling to reconcile our deep inner pain
with our outer comfort. *And it just doesn't work.*

Jeff says he expected money to make him a good
man. He felt that providing more and more for himself
and his family was the core of his existence. "I completely ignored everything else," he says. "I never turned
down an opportunity to make money. It seemed like
that was the only thing that mattered, and it justified
anything. I gradually stopped thinking about anything
else. I manipulated money and made it turn into more
money. It felt exciting and powerful—all that buying
and selling. It was just like playing Monopoly for real."

When Jeff began having problems with his marriage,
his clients, and his boss, he reacted angrily. "I couldn't

understand why everyone was hassling me," he says. "I was making them all so much money. What else could possibly matter? What could they possibly have to complain about? I really thought I was great as long as I kept making more and more money, and it didn't matter how I did it or what else I was or wasn't doing. It wasn't until I lost everything—my wife, my family, my job— that I could stand back and look at the way I'd let the pursuit of money take over my whole life."

Good Guys—Bad Guys

Like Jeff, many of us may have developed a belief that *good guys are rich and bad guys are poor*. This kind of attitude may have originated in our families, neighborhoods, or culture at large when we were growing up. "Success" may always have meant monetary gain. The people we admired, whether real or fictional, may have been wealthy—or at least wealthier than we were.

Believing that happiness requires wealth may have grown naturally out of an attitude we picked up about rich people being somehow *better* than the rest of us. They may have been envied, copied, or revered as superior. They may have been seen as *above* the rest of the world and its cares, problems, and pain. They may have been our heroes.

Conversely, poor people may have been presented to us as dirty, lazy, and evil. We may have learned to fear and hate those who had less than we did. We may have grown to believe in fictional images of poor people as lacking in education, intelligence, manners, cleanliness, health, and morals. We may have learned to blame and judge them for their situations.

These beliefs and attitudes may lie quietly beneath our feelings about money, and their effect on our own self-image. If we have problems with money, we feel it means we're *bad* somehow; if we have good luck or success, we see it as proof that we're *good*. Measuring our own goodness and worth by our monetary success can become a one-way road to depression, anxiety, fear, and self-hate. It can be our ego's way of keeping us locked in unhappiness.

Fairy Tales

All the fairy tales I can remember from childhood ended with someone living happily ever after in a castle or palace or someplace like that. Poor little barefoot— but sweet and selfless—girls ended up princesses, while mean, selfish creeps—if they survived—ended up poor, wretched beggars. In our childhood fantasies, we don't dream of growing up to become paupers.

This attitude that money and luxurious comfort equals happiness may have become firmly planted in our minds. Even if other factors in our early environment taught us otherwise, that element may live on in our beliefs, unconsciously. We may expect to be rescued someday by a rich prince who will make us perfectly and permanently happy. We may expect years of self-sacrifice and hard work to be rewarded with luxurious wealth and corresponding joy.

The realities of adult life may seem cruel and unfair compared to these childhood fantasies. We may become angry and bitter when money and luxury don't make us happy after all. Or we may spend our whole lives waiting, planning, wishing, and scheming for our dream to come true.

Acceptance of reality is maturity. Turning to our spirit's true vision and away from our ego's fantasies and fairy tales allows us to finally find true joy, happiness, and peace. The problem isn't that we haven't yet found our pot of gold at the end of the rainbow—it's that we spend our time and energy looking for it, while true happiness is right under our noses all along.

As far as our real, true, inner happiness is concerned, money just doesn't matter. As Joseph Campbell said in *The Power of Myth,* "There is something inside you that knows when you're in the center, that knows when you're on the beam and when you're off the beam. And if you get off the beam to earn money, you've lost your life. And if you stay in the center and don't have any money, you still have your bliss." We know that our true happiness, or what Joseph Campbell called "bliss," comes from within our deepest spiritual selves, not from any outer circumstance or condition. When we stay focused on our spiritual centers, the financial conditions of our lives have little effect on our inner states of mind.

Hating Money

Hugh Prather writes, "The ancient wisdom that the love of money is behind much of the evil of the world is true. And so, too, are the hate and fear of money." Hate and fear of money can become our rationale for losing, mishandling, or being unable to get any. We may blame money itself for our difficulty in obtaining, keeping, or using it wisely. We may feel resentful and angry toward those who have more than we do, and judge them "evil" in some way.

We may also feel guilty for having plenty of money. We may deny ourselves or our families things we could easily afford because of a deep belief that it's only okay to have money if we don't enjoy it. We may deny or cover up our wealth, feeling embarrassed or ashamed of it.

Andrea says she grew up watching her mother struggle to make ends meet. She explains, "As a single mother with four children to raise and not even a high school diploma, she worked and worked and worked some more, just to put food on the table. She was a smart, hardworking, loving, moral woman who just never got a break in life. I saw the struggle for money make her old before her time, but I always loved and respected her. I thought those other people out there for whom everything seemed so easy were contemptible."

As an adult, Andrea found herself unable to accept or enjoy monetary success. She felt guilty for making so much more money than her mother ever had. She took low-paying jobs and worked longer hours than necessary. She says, "In my mind, my mother was a saint. How could I grow up to be one of those evil people who didn't slave and sacrifice all the time? It just didn't seem right to have it so much better than she had."

We may also develop a similar hate of money if our family was wealthy. If we had painful or difficult relationships with our parents and they were financially well-off, we may associate money with what we see as our parents' faults. We may rebel against them by rejecting their viewpoint on money or their level of income. We may wish to distance ourselves from everything they valued.

Bad Guys—Good Guys

While growing up, we may have developed an attitude that *bad guys are rich and good guys are poor.* If our heroes were the downtrodden, oppressed, and poor, we may find it hard to accept abundance in our lives as adults. If wealth was seen as somehow evil, or wealthy people were seen as the oppressors, we may

135

understandably not want to identify ourselves with these negative images.

We may feel we need to remain poor in order to feel good about ourselves. We may—perhaps unconsciously—sabotage our opportunities for financial gain. In our minds, we may associate guilt and anger with money. We may feel like one of the "bad guys" if we start making too much money or having too much material comfort.

If we see large companies or institutions as "rich bad guys," we may feel justified in such practices as not paying our bills on time or finding ways to get out of paying what we owe them. "Oh, they can afford it," may be our excuse for unethical or even illegal practices. We may even feel a certain satisfaction in cheating someone or some company we view as one of the wealthy bad guys.

Our ego easily becomes embroiled in this game of blame and defend. Being one of the good guys may be our justification for any action against one of the bad guys. We may say we hate money and all the big systems and people who we think control it, and therefore keep ourselves ignorant of handling it in a way that enhances our own best interests.

Fear of Money

All hate grows out of fear. We may fear money because we don't know anything about it. We may fear money because we think having it makes us one of the bad guys. We may fear money because we don't believe we deserve it. Fear is our ego's favorite exercise, and it can keep us ignorant, poor, angry, guilty, and deprived.

Letting go of our fear requires a realistic perspective on money as a tool for the exchange of goods and services—nothing more, nothing less. A fearless attitude toward money allows us to begin taking responsibility for our finances in a healthy, happy way. It frees us from the ego games of worshipping or hating money, blaming others or money itself for our problems with it, and expecting money to solve our problems and make us happy.

Scarcity Beliefs

One of the deeply held beliefs that keep us from handling money with ease is that of scarcity and lack. We may believe there simply isn't enough to go around. We may accept our ego's view that whatever we have is depriving someone else, and what they have is depriving us.

This attitude divides humanity into the *haves* and the *have-nots*. The haves must feel guilty, and the have-nots must feel angry. There can never be a relaxed attitude of sharing and equitable distribution in this viewpoint. Anyone's gain is always someone else's loss. This is the ego's hopeless, defensive viewpoint. But what else can we believe when it seems so hard to get ahead financially, or even to just make ends meet?

Many of us have always felt that we were "just getting by"—barely able to pay the essential bills and keep ourselves and our families fed. We may live from one paycheck to the next, perhaps with some very lean days before the next check is due. We may pay only some of our bills one month, and the others the next, hoping someday to get caught up with them all. We may continue in this manner even as our income increases. We may develop habits of living just barely within our means, no matter how those means grow.

Sometimes we may feel so trapped by the scarcity of money that we can't spend what we have. We may feel paralyzed by the possibility of making mistakes. If a dinner gets ruined or we don't like the taste, we may feel terribly guilty for throwing it away. We may feel a deep sense of loss over a stained shirt or broken dish. We may feel that we can't afford to be imperfect.

One woman says, "It's like I can't take any risks, because there's just no room for error. So I don't buy anything I don't absolutely need, and then I buy the cheapest one I can find. That way, if it gets lost, broken, or whatever, I don't feel quite so bad." This feeling comes from our belief in money as a finite resource, which must always be sought after anew, whenever we let go of any.

Changing Our Attitudes

On the surface, scarcity may seem to be a realistic view of the world. There are finite resources that need to be used carefully and replenished. But it is well within human capabilities to do this in a responsible way. And new resources are always being discovered. There is no limit in sight to the expansion of human knowledge and ingenuity.

There is also no limit to our spirit's capacity for sharing and generosity. Only our ego feels threatened by the idea of finite resources. Our spirit knows the universe is unlimited and abundant. This knowledge allows our spirits to be completely secure and fearless.

If we feel that we just don't make enough money for the things we really need, we can get help. Financial advisors can assist us in planning a budget, paying off our debts, and managing our money in the best possible way. There may be many more options available to us than we ever imagined. But we can't learn about all the possibilities unless we seek and accept the help we need.

Our ego's games of false pride, ignorance, anger, and a self-image as a *have-not* only create self-defeating attitudes and behaviors. But we can turn to another viewpoint. We can let go of our false beliefs in a world of lack and scarcity, of *haves* and *have-nots*. We can open ourselves up to the infinite abundance of the universe.

Deprivation Beliefs

Sometimes we stop ourselves from receiving all the good things that can come to us by simply believing, on a deep, perhaps unconscious level, that we don't deserve them. We may have old negative programming telling us that all those good things we want are for others, not us. When we were growing up, we may never have seen an important adult in our lives set a goal, work toward it, and achieve it.

Our self-image has to change if we are going to allow ourselves to accept abundance and financial ease. This doesn't necessarily mean wealth; it means dealing with money in a relaxed way, free of anxiety and stress. It means accepting good things coming to us through the natural flow of positive energy in the world. It means getting out of our own way.

Even if wonderful things are available to us right now, we can't see or accept them if we feel undeserving. As Melody Beattie writes in her book, *Beyond Codependency*, "Deprived, negative thinking makes things disappear." We sabotage our opportunities for abundance when we refuse to see ourselves as deserving. Our ego keeps us thinking this way, convinced it is protecting

139

us from disappointment and rejection. But in reality, it is only keeping us stuck in misery and lack.

Spring Break

When he was growing up in Michigan, Nate says all his friends went to Florida for spring break. His parents always said they couldn't afford such a trip, and he felt guilty for wishing he could go. In college, Nate worked, but never seemed to be able to save enough money to go along with his friends on their annual trip.

Nate says, "Even now, after years of working and being on my own, I never go anywhere for vacation. It just doesn't seem to fit into my budget no matter how much money I make. When I get time off from work, I spend it working around my house or just relaxing at home. It's like I have this mental block about going away for a vacation—it just doesn't seem like *me*."

Nate's self-image, formed when he was growing up, includes staying home while his friends all go away on vacation. It's what he's used to, what has come to feel appropriate to him. It has nothing to do with whether he can actually afford to go or not. It has only to do with his attitudes and beliefs.

Often, when something is outside our self-image, we can't even see our opportunities for doing it. We may say or think, *Who, me? Buy a new car? Own a home? Go away on vacation?* We may not even think these thoughts consciously, but just have an uncomfortable feeling about stepping beyond the boundaries of our deprived self-image.

A New Self-Image

Learning to see ourselves as deserving of all the good things in life doesn't mean indulging every little whim or desire we may have. It doesn't mean buying a lot of things we don't need or really even want just to puff out our chests and say, "I deserve it." It means letting go of our mistaken self-image as someone who can't have the things he or she needs and wants. It means letting go of our delusions about being somehow less deserving of money than others.

Sometimes accepting something we need or want means sacrificing for a while in order to save up for it. Sometimes it means choosing between one thing and another, when we can only afford one. These are not the same as self-imposed deprivation because they are reasonable, temporary, and help us get something good for ourselves in the end.

When we let go of our ego's self-image as undeserving or incapable of financial abundance and ease, we can begin letting abundance flow into our lives. We can let go of grasping onto things we don't really want except to assuage our ego's deprived feeling, and accept the things that really do enhance our well-being. We can let our spirits be calm, peaceful, happy, and abundant.

Inflowing and Outflowing of Money

In his play, *The Matchmaker,* Thornton Wilder wrote, "Money is like manure; it's not worth a thing unless it's spread around encouraging young things to grow." Money must flow, circulate around throughout the community, in order to keep trade moving and people supplied with the things they need and want. If we hoard our money, we cut ourselves off from the flow and begin to stagnate.

In order to open ourselves both to the inflowing and the outflowing of money, the first thing we must do is *learn* about it. A husband who says, "Oh, my wife pays all the bills," or a wife who says, "My husband handles all that sort of thing," is giving away a huge part of life. Becoming more knowledgeable about money is more than just paying the bills or balancing the checkbook; it's understanding money and its role in our lives. It's taking care of ourselves and our personal power and responsibility.

Spouses and partners can learn these things together, or trade off so that both learn all aspects of finances. We *all* need to learn about bank accounts, interest, credit, taxes, and everything that affects our personal finances. If we don't, we can't make the best choices and decisions regarding money, and we can't clear out all our negative and incorrect beliefs about money. This clearing out is necessary for a smooth flow of money into and out of our lives.

The smooth flow of money makes it possible for us to focus our energies elsewhere. As Hugh Prather writes, "Money is not important; therefore, do whatever allows you not to be preoccupied with it." To let go of our preoccupation with money, we have to learn everything we need to know about it; examine our feelings toward it; let go of our old beliefs, assumptions, and fears about it; and start letting it flow smoothly into and out of our lives.

Inflowing

Inflowing means accepting the money that can come to us. To do this we need to let go of any old beliefs, such as we don't deserve money or can't have enough money to live well. It also means letting go of resentment against others who we think have more than we do, and adopting an attitude of generosity and abundance toward everyone. It means knowing that wealth won't make us happy and poverty won't make us saints.

In order to open ourselves to all the possible inflowing of abundance, we have to let go of our feelings of anger, resentment, guilt, and fear. We have to give up our scarcity beliefs and open our minds to the idea of infinite abundance in the universe. We also have to accept the notion that this infinite abundance is here as much for us as anyone else. We have to stop worshipping or hating money, and recognize its true role in this world.

When we let go of our delusions about ourselves, the world, and money, we can begin enjoying our money without guilt, anxiety, fear, or miserly behavior. We can begin appreciating our money and the things it buys for us. We can become grateful and allow money to flow smoothly into our lives.

Outflowing

Outflowing is just as important as inflowing to keep the supply of monetary energy moving. We need to let go of all the old things we don't need. The meditation book, *God Calling,* tells us, "When supply seems to have failed . . . look around to see what you can give away. Give away something. There is always a stagnation, a blockage, when supply seems short. Your giving clears that away." Go through all your things and give away anything that doesn't fit you or you have no more use for. A good rule of thumb is to give away anything you haven't used in the past year—that usually indicates that you will probably never use it again.

We often feel quite afraid to let go of our things like this. Especially if we have experienced times of poverty and lack in the past, we may feel somehow protected by possessing things, even if we never use them. But letting them go really is the best way to keep the energy flowing, to make room for new things to come to us. If we are not using the things we have, they are only blocking our ability to help others and receive more good for ourselves. If we give them away, other people can make use of them, and the flow keeps moving through us to others and so on.

Money itself can flow in the same manner as material things. Whenever we pay our bills, or buy things we need at the store, or give money to charity, we are contributing to the flow. I'm not advocating wild spending or credit debt—we are always responsible for using our money sensibly. But we often stop ourselves from buying things we can afford because of our fears about not getting any more money once we spend what we've got.

Abundance Thinking

When Joseph Campbell returned from Europe as a student in 1929, the stock market crashed and jobs were scarce for the next five years. Yet he said, "That was a great time for me. I didn't feel poor. I just felt that I didn't have any money."

Has there ever been a time when you felt truly, completely, blissfully happy, regardless of your financial circumstances? Perhaps you were in love, or gave birth to a child, or recovered from an illness. Perhaps your mind was totally absorbed in something greater than yourself—a social or political cause, or another person's welfare. Perhaps you were so fully focused on learning—whether in school, on a job, or in your relationships—that you forgot about money for a while.

These times can teach us how to let go of our ego's grasping, insatiable drive for monetary gain. They can remind us that happiness has nothing to do with money. They can help us to relax and trust in the abundance of the universe, which comes to us when we're concentrating our energies on what we need to do and learn in the world.

"God will provide."

Marvin says, "I used to be completely caught up in making money. It was the most important thing in my life. Everything I did, every decision I made, was in some way connected to making more and more money. I thought I was just doing what everybody was or should be doing to live a good life, to get ahead.

"I had some friends," Marvin continues, "who were always just getting by. I thought they were stupid, even *crazy* for the decisions they made—decisions based on things like feelings, intuitions, and moral ideals. I figured that was all well and good, but business was business. When I tried to talk some sense into them, they just smiled and said things like, 'God will provide.' That's when I really thought they were nuts. But they kept on getting by, and after a while, they did quite well for themselves. Now they have a beautiful family and a beautiful home, and they're the happiest people I know."

When we see the world as a beautiful, abundant place, with plenty for everyone, that's what it can become. Faith and trust in our Higher Power and our own ability to make a positive contribution to the world and to be part of the flow of energy can make it happen. This is what it means to have an attitude of abundance— to see the world from the loving viewpoint of our spirit,

Choosing Happiness

which knows that there is always enough to go around. We just have to free up our minds and let it happen.

What Does It Mean to Live Abundantly?

Living abundantly doesn't mean acquiring everything we possibly can. Such compulsive consumption only indicates fear and confused thinking about money. We each have to determine for ourselves what things we need and want. But we should always examine *why* we want things.

Do you feel a need to impress others or some old critical voices in your mind? Do you feel that more money will protect you from painful relationships or problems? Is money a substitute for resolving conflicts in other areas of your life? Or, are you depriving yourself out of fear of loss or an undeserving self-image? Do you believe there is not really enough to go around? Do you believe that having possessions or success deprives others of similar good things? Do you believe that others' success deprives you of the same?

Whether we over- or underindulge our need for money and material things, our egos are calling the shots. When we find our own level of balance, using our spirit's guidance and values, we can discover a comfortable flow of abundance in our lives.

The Middle Way

Our spirit's viewpoint is one of neutrality regarding money. It can neither hate nor worship money, because it knows money isn't really important. But it *is* something we have to deal with in this world, and it's not going to go away any time soon. So the loving, spiritual viewpoint is to take care of it as best we can, so that we can turn our attention to other things.

146

Plato wrote, "Wealth is the parent of luxury and indolence, and poverty of meanness and viciousness, and both of discontent." The Buddha taught the "Middle Way"—that extremes of either wealth or poverty are not the best ways for people to live. Only when money is not the central focus of our lives, one way or the other, can we stand back and see it as it truly is, and let it take its rightful place in our lives.

The right place for money to be in our lives is wherever we don't have to think about it much. We need enough of it to live on, to provide ourselves and our families with food, clothing, and shelter. We need what we need—no more, no less. Comfort is reasonable, luxury tends to take over and require too much of our attention.

These judgments are, of course, relative. And we will need to make certain distinctions for ourselves. But the main thing we need to remember is that money is not important at all in itself. As Hugh Prather writes, "Unlike people, money is what money does." When we use money as a tool to create things like education, food, health, shelter, comfort, kindness, caring, and assistance to others, it becomes a part of the natural flow of love and positive energy in the world. And it can't serve any better purpose than that.

Exercises

Exercise One

Learn About Money. Learn all you can in order to gain a realistic perspective on money and to help you manage yours. Take courses, ask questions, read all the material your banks, insurance companies, and other financial institutions send you. Find out about bank accounts, interest rates, taxes, credit, and insurance policies to gain a full understanding of all your options and choices. Examine your bills and try to understand them completely. Call the company if you have questions. Find a financial advisor if you need help with budgeting and managing your money.

Exercise Two

Outflowing. Go through all of your belongings and give away anything you're not using. Give a few cans of food to your local food bank. Drop a few cents into the Salvation Army bucket every time you pass one at Christmastime. When you see a box next to a cash register asking for a donation for a charitable cause, drop your change into it. Give a few dollars every payday to a community service organization. Do these kinds of things on a regular basis until they become a habit.

CHAPTER NINE

Health and Aging

It just goes to show you—it's always something.

—Gilda Radner

Comedienne Gilda Radner died at the age of forty-two after a two-year struggle with ovarian cancer. Her book, *It's Always Something,* describes the hope, courage, and humor with which she faced that struggle. It also describes her fear, anger, and pain.

Chronic, debilitating, or potentially life-threatening illness can evoke all of these responses, and more. Our bodies can grab our attention with pain and disability, forcing us to face new challenges. We are *challenged to change* our behavioral habits, our self-image, our beliefs and attitudes. We are *challenged to choose* how we will cope with these changes and whether we accept or resist them. We are challenged to find and maintain our inner peace and happiness, regardless of our body's condition.

It *Is* Always Something

We don't often think about sickness as normal or even healthy. But the human body is designed to get sick and frequently does. As Paul Pearsall writes, "Disease is healthy, a normal part of living that does not mean you have failed in any way." Many of us get stuck in denying our illness rather than accepting it, and become unable to learn from it. Acceptance doesn't mean resigning ourselves to dismal predictions for our future; it means living fully every moment of every day, even if that moment brings ill health or disability. It means recognizing and living with that physical reality, instead of ignoring or denying it.

We can all learn to accept ourselves physically, no matter what challenges we face. But first we have to examine our views on illness and disability. We have to clear out all our resistance to the reality of imperfect health. We have to recognize the attitudes and beliefs that keep us stuck in fear and denial. We have to give up unrealistic expectations of ourselves and our bodies.

The Quest for Perfection

Our culture worships perfect health and fitness. Any deviation from the mass media image of strength, endurance, and a full range of physical abilities is often seen as deficient, and we may feel shame and self-blame for these less-than-perfect characteristics. We may try to deny or cover up our real, human limitations. We may spend enormous amounts of time and energy pursuing an ideal of health and fitness.

We may give up alcohol, cigarettes, red meat, caffeine, salt, and sugar. We may jog, swim, play sports, do aerobics, and meditate. We may drink mineral water and eat low-fat, high fiber, low-cholesterol foods. You'd think that eventually we'd get to the point of living perfectly and feeling perfect all the time. But it doesn't seem to work that way. As Gilda Radner said, "It's always something," and we may react to that reality as we react to Murphy's Law, with anger and resentment.

Perfection isn't possible in the area of health any more than it is possible in any other area of life. We can't control that reality. We *can* control our reactions to it. We can accept that our bodies need a certain amount of attention in the form of exercise, rest, and nutrition, but that even the best care in these areas won't guarantee complete freedom from illness, pain, injury, or disability. We can learn to live happily and fully with the realities of our imperfect bodies.

Playing Hurt

One of the ways we often try to deny and control our bodies is by pushing ourselves to perform physically, even when we aren't feeling well. Athletes who compete with injuries or illnesses are admired and congratulated for their commitment and perseverance. Even if the choice compounds their illness or injury, it is considered a worthwhile self-sacrifice for the sake of the game or the team.

Roger's friend, Calvin, was the star player on his high school basketball team. Roger says, "We'd been on the team together since our freshman year, but we'd played at the park and in our driveways since we were little kids. We loved the game and were really proud to go to a school that went to state every year. Our senior season was the best we'd ever played, and we were really excited for the championship finals.

"But at the time of the final games, Calvin had been fighting off the Hong Kong flu, which was going around that year. He didn't miss any games, even though he'd really been sick off and on for weeks. He didn't look good, but he said he felt okay for the last big game. He played in the game, scored several points, we won, and he left the gym in an ambulance. He never regained consciousness and died a couple of days later."

Roger says Calvin's death affected his attitude toward sports. "I'd always thought it was cool to play hurt," he says. "It meant you were tough and committed and dependable. But I didn't feel that way anymore. Calvin's funeral was a big school affair. He was a real hero. He had literally given his life for the school basketball team. It was ridiculous. It was just plain *stupid* for him to have played in that game. So what if he couldn't play because he had the flu? I'd have given anything to have Calvin back—that was all that mattered."

A Course in Miracles tells us to "recognize what does not matter." Our ego often convinces us that many things are more important than taking care of our health: prestige, championships, and our self-image as tough and perfect. In retrospect, it's easy to see that Calvin's health was far more important than any basketball game. But how often do we wait until it's too late to face the realities of our physical limitations? How often do we go to work with a cold or flu? Do we think about the possibility of making ourselves worse or of infecting our co-workers? Do we recognize our inability to perform at our best when we aren't feeling well? Do we feel exalted in our self-sacrifice, or resentful for our perception that others *expect* us to show up, no matter what? Adults should be able to determine when they are and are not up to working, socializing, or traveling. Taking responsibility for ourselves must include knowing how and when to say no.

Illness

Sometimes we get hit with an illness we can't ignore. Our body gives out on us in an unmistakable way. We

know something is wrong, and after trying unsuccess-
fully to deny or ignore it, we are forced to face it. This
is often when we begin trying to control it. We may go
to the doctor, expecting a quick cure. We may temporarily alter our behaviors, expecting preventive mea-
sures to reverse a physical condition already present.
We may try making bargains with God.

Magical thinking may be our response before we
come to terms with the reality of our physical condition.
We may persist in unrealistic expectations, afraid to face
the truth. We may cling stubbornly to our delusions and
pretenses, rather than learning to live with the condition
in the best way possible. We may put off acceptance
and growth through the experience of illness for as long
as we can.

Illness is a reality of life. All of us, at some time, will
experience it. Sometimes it comes and goes quickly,
while other times it may last for years. Sometimes its
symptoms come and go sporadically, and other times
we are constantly reminded of it by pain or disability.
Illness can take our physical abilities, our comfort, and
even our body's life. The challenge is not to let it take
our ability to experience peace and joy.

Children and Illness

Children seem to deal with chronic, traumatic, or
disabling physical conditions better than adults. They
don't seem to spend as much time and energy on
self-blame, anger, hopelessness, worry, and resentment
over all the things they can't do. Children are resilient
and accepting. If we've had a physical condition since
childhood, such as diabetes, we'll probably have far less
trouble dealing with it as adults because we're used to
it; it's become a way of life. But when we are hit with

something new in adulthood, we often resist the change.

We can learn from children living with illnesses and disabilities, and we can also discover the child within ourselves, who is always ready to face reality and adapt to it. We can find hope, courage, faith, and humor with which to open ourselves up to new experiences. We can let go of beliefs that we need certain physical attributes and capabilities in order to find peace and happiness. We can focus our attention on living fully from day to day and moment to moment, as children do.

Our Self-Image

A large part of our difficulty in accepting physical changes may be our self-image. We are not our bodies, illnesses, or disabilities. We are still and always human beings with dignity, integrity, and worth. We deserve respect and understanding, even from ourselves. Illness needn't take over our identity. We are always ourselves, no matter what changes our bodies might go through.

Gilda Radner wrote that after months of various treatments, including chemotherapy and its resulting hair loss, she began introducing herself by saying, "I used to be Gilda Radner." She explained, "That was how I felt. I used to be her, but now I was someone else." Being someone with an illness or disability isn't a substitute for being who we are. We may sometimes feel as if our illness has taken over, but it is within our power to reclaim our own personal identity as a whole human being.

Accepting Help

Having to accept help may not feel very good to us at first, but it can be a tremendous learning experience.

It can bring us closer to others and offer us opportunities to help them by letting them feel helpful and competent. It is only our ego's false pride and fear of dependency that make accepting help hard for us. Sometimes we need to learn to do things for ourselves, but learning when it's appropriate to accept help from others is a big step toward letting go of our false self-image as perfect.

We aren't perfect. Sometimes we need help. Sometimes we feel pain. Sometimes we can't physically do everything we'd like to. Sometimes we need to learn new ways of living, getting around, seeing, hearing, speaking, or performing other physical tasks. The one thing we never need to learn over again is *being*. We always have within us a place of perfect calm, peace, love, and acceptance. This center of our true self can always be found, no matter what is going on with our bodies. We can go to this place whenever the outer conditions of our physical selves are in pain or distress. It may not make the discomfort or difficulty go away, but it will remind us of who we really are, and bring us back to our spiritual center.

Chronic Conditions

Corinne has suffered from migraine headaches for as long as she can remember. She has tried all kinds of drugs, dietary restrictions, and relaxation techniques to prevent and control them, but she still gets them. She says, "Some of the things I've tried seem to have helped me get the headaches less frequently, but nothing has stopped them altogether, and nothing really stops the pain effectively once I get one.

"For people who have never had a migraine headache, there's probably nothing I can say to accurately describe one," Corinne continues. "The pain is unlike anything else, and I'm pretty useless when I have one. I can't work, I can't deal with other people, and I can't stand light or noise. Lying down in a darkened room is about all I can do, and even that doesn't feel good.

"In the past, I have tried ignoring the migraines, willing them away, relaxing them away, and drugging them away. I have forced myself to go on with my normal activities, and I have tolerated people saying silly things like, 'Have you tried taking aspirin?'

"Now I've learned to live with my migraines, to recognize when one is coming on, to accept it and do what I have to do about it. I try to do whatever might help them occur less frequently, but I know I'll probably keep having them from time to time, and I accept that. When they happen, I'll do whatever I have to do to get through them, and they'll be gone when they're gone. I don't get upset about it, and I don't expect a miracle cure. I've learned to accept this reality and deal with it. It's just a normal part of my life—a small part of my life."

We can learn to live with any chronic physical condition, if we first admit that we have it, then learn all we can about it, do what we can to minimize its negative effects, and accept it without anger, self-blame, or magical thinking. Whether it's hearing or vision loss, diabetes, premenstrual syndrome, migraine headaches, or whatever, we can take the positive action that is within our power and let go of what we have no control over.

This means being an active participant in our treatment. Our doctor can write a prescription for us, but we have to get it filled, take it properly, watch for results, including side effects, and report them back to our doctor. Our doctor can say we need regular exercise, but *we* have to find a form of exercise that fits into our schedule and lifestyle, and *do* it. Our doctor can recommend dietary changes, but *we're* the only ones who put food into our mouths.

Hearing the Messages

We're also the only one who lives inside our body. We have to become sensitive to our body and the messages it has for us. For example, Corinne has noticed what seems to be a correlation between her migraine headaches and sugar. She says, "I don't need a million-dollar university study proving that sugar consumption can trigger a migraine. I just avoid sugar. It's no big deal, just something I've noticed, and consequently, I've done something positive about it. Maybe it wouldn't work for someone else, but it does seem to help me, so I do it."

If you ate something new and it made you violently ill, you probably wouldn't eat it again. The human body often gives us such clear messages when something isn't good for us. But sometimes the messages are more subtle, and we have to listen harder. Sometimes illness is a way of forcing us to relax, slow down, change our eating habits, get more rest, or stop some harmful behavior. Sometimes it can help us get a whole new perspective on life and what's really important to us. Sometimes it can open us up to all kinds of talents, abilities, and characteristics we never knew we possessed.

One thing to remember about listening to our body's messages is not to use it as an excuse for self-blame or worry. For example, it won't help us to get upset and beat ourselves up for not eating properly in the past. Instead, we can take our body's messages about food and begin eating more healthy foods *now*. We can also remember not to search frantically for a reason or somewhere to place blame for our physical problems. Sometimes we just can't see a reason, and that's okay. Blaming ourselves or others never helps anyone. We just have to be open to the wisdom our body can teach us, but not manufacture messages to fit our ego's sense of guilt and defensiveness.

Impairments

Specific physical impairments require specific changes in our behaviors and habits. Learning to use a walker, a wheelchair, or a prosthetic device of some kind can mean the difference between mobility and immobility, dependence and independence. Impairments mean that we must open up to doing things *differently*. We are challenged to fulfill all of our needs and accomplish all we can in whatever ways we can. So what if they aren't the ways other people do them or the ways we used to do them?

The accomplishments of people like Helen Keller (*The Miracle Worker*) and Christy Brown (*My Left Foot*) despite their disabilities are well known. Not so well known are the thousands upon thousands of others who have faced impairments of all kinds and learned to live fully with them. When we must learn to live with a disability, these people can provide invaluable help and understanding. Just as recovering alcoholics, drug addicts, and others share their experiences and help in support groups, so can disabled persons help each other.

One of the hardest parts of learning to live with impairments can be other people's reactions. Unfortunately, we have not yet reached a time when other people's disabilities never trigger our ego's fear and defensiveness. So we may feel confused and unsure of how to act when we encounter someone with an impairment. We wonder if we should offer help or if this would be insulting. We wonder if we should talk about the obvious disability or pretend not to notice it. We wonder if asking questions would be rude, even though it might help us to understand better. Even with the best of intentions, we may behave badly when faced with someone else's disability.

We are moving toward the day when handicap awareness will be commonplace, and impaired people will be able to move about in our world unobstructed. Already, handicap accessibility is being built into our public buildings, and awareness is growing. As these changes evolve, we can all learn and grow in our understanding. Eventually, education and experience will make us all more aware and accepting of the reality of physical impairments. Right now, we need to be patient and understanding with ourselves and each other, while making an effort to bridge the gap of communication between us.

Physical impairments can only limit our physical abilities. Our spirit is unaffected by anything that goes on in our body. It is a calm, peaceful oasis deep within ourselves. It can remind us to let go of our old stubborn viewpoints and adapt joyfully to whatever comes our way. It can lead us gently away from our ego's fear, anger, and self-blame. It can fill us with courage, hope, faith, and acceptance.

Feeling What You Feel
Illness and disability challenge our emotions. We may go through phases of anger, sadness, fear, doubt, depression, self-pity, blame, grief, and hopelessness. This

is normal and to be expected. What we are challenged to do is work at the things we can change, and accept those that we can't.

Even after we feel we've adapted to our condition, we may have moods or times when we feel upset or down about it. We may grow tired of treatments, therapies, exercises, or pain. We may feel resentful or envious of others who we think have it easier than we do. We may let our ego run wild occasionally, filling us with worry or fear. But these times don't have to last forever, and we can be understanding and gentle enough with ourselves to see them for what they are.

Gilda Radner wrote, "I always found that after a really good cry, I felt better about everything. I felt as though I got rid of some toxicity, that I got rid of some of the pain and the mourning." Having a good cry once in a while is okay; it's even good for us. It's only when we find ourselves crying—literally or figuratively—*all the time,* that we need to examine our approach to our illness or impairment and maybe get help to change that.

Feelings are normal, natural, and healthy, as long as we remember that we can choose not to let them take over and stop us from finding deep peace and happiness. Instead, we can accept them, understand them, and let them go. As Martha Cleveland writes in her book, *The Twelve Step Response to Chronic Illness and Disability,* "We can outmaneuver the effects of our physical illness with spiritual wellness."

Spiritual Wellness

Learning to live fully and happily with illness or disability requires focus on our inner strengths and wisdom. It grows out of our spiritual awareness and understanding. It comes from our spirit's ability to face any outer condition with peace and joy. It begins with our acceptance of the things we cannot change, and our effort to change the things we can.

Since I believe our spirits are always perfect, I define spiritual wellness as the open, healthy relationship between our conscious mind and our inner being. This relationship allows our spiritual wisdom, peacefulness, love, joy, and acceptance to radiate into our everyday thoughts, behaviors, and feelings. It is the conscious choice to look through the eyes of our spirit rather than our ego. It is a loving way to think of our physical beings, including hope; active participation in our treatment, recovery, or adaptation to disability; finding the good in every experience; learning and growing from every experience; and celebrating life, whatever physical challenges it presents.

Hope

In his book, *Peace, Love, & Healing,* Bernie Siegel writes, "There is no false hope, there is only false *no-hope,* because we can't predict the future of an individual." No one really can predict our future. Doctors can make estimates based on past experience, but they never absolutely know what course a disease will take. New treatments are being discovered every day, and our state of mind can always increase our chances for recovery.

But hope doesn't necessarily mean believing we will recover our previous health or physical abilities. Healing doesn't always mean curing disease. It can mean finding balance in all areas of our life. It can mean discovering our inner self, our center, our spirit. It can mean peace, love, joy, and tranquility, *regardless* of what's happening to us physically.

161

Hope is simply a positive attitude, an optimistic viewpoint on ourselves and our life. It can mean facing each day with joy and peace and love. It can mean experiencing each moment openly and allowing ourselves to be changed. It can mean facing each new challenge as it comes with a balance of effort, optimism, and acceptance.

Active Participation

Our own participation is the most important element of any treatment or therapy of any kind. We cannot turn ourselves over to medical personnel or technology or caregivers and expect to be "fixed." We are *there,* present and all-important to whatever is going on. We need to get our minds and hearts into our own treatment, therapy, exercise, or whatever needs to be done about our illness or disability. We need to accept what we can't control, but we also need to *do* what we *can.*

In her book, Gilda Radner told of a woman who kissed each of her pills before she took them. She put *love* into her treatment, embracing medical science as her partner in recovery. We can put this same kind of love into every action we can take in dealing with our illness or disability. We can stop thinking about what we can't do, and concentrate on the joy and wonder of all we *can.* We can love ourselves and all the aspects of our bodies, lives, and spirits.

Active participation may mean asking questions and learning all we can about our illness or disability. It may mean making the effort to get in touch with others who have already been through what we're facing for the first time. It may mean learning to make specific changes in our living habits. It may mean doing difficult physical therapy exercises or learning to use new equipment. It may mean doing a lot of *internal* work, perhaps not to regain our physical abilities, but to rediscover our ability to experience love, peace, and joy.

Finding the Good

How can we find anything good about pain, illness, or the loss of physical abilities? What could possibly be good about losing our vision, hearing, freedom of movement, or an actual part of our body? These challenges may seem completely negative in themselves, but when we experience them, we often discover positive side effects or by-products that we couldn't have found any other way.

Martha Cleveland writes, "Somehow the loss of complete health or full physical function shakes us up and our priorities settle in a different order." We are changed by illness or disability in ways we may never have imagined. We may suddenly realize what is truly important to us. We may discover strength and discipline and accomplishment far greater than we've ever experienced. We may proceed to live a life of greater love, peace, joy, and happiness than we've ever thought possible.

Illness or disability can be seen as a second chance— a chance to re-examine our lives and our priorities, a chance to rediscover who we really are. We may never be the same again—and that may be the best thing that could happen.

Learning and Growing

There are so many lessons within the experiences of illness and disability that any discussion here will necessarily be incomplete. Each of us, individually, discovers what we need to learn through our own experiences. The lessons of a specific illness or impairment may be completely different from one person to another. But enormous opportunities for learning and growing are always present in every experience of illness or disability.

Some lessons seem to be shared by many people, such as learning to focus on the present, rather than worrying about the past or the future; learning to let go of things we can't control; accepting the help we need; and thinking about the non-physical aspects of our being, possibly for the first time. Martha Cleveland writes, "Without facing the realities of impairment, it's easier to deny spiritual development and spend our energy chasing physical perfection."

The challenges of physical illness or impairment force us to look at many things in a new way. This in itself can cause mental, emotional, and spiritual growth. Realizing that there is another way to look at anything allows our consciousness to turn from our ego's to our spirit's viewpoint. Without the illness or disability, we may never have changed our outlook or discovered our spirituality.

Celebrating Life

Albert Schweitzer wrote, "Affirmation of life is the spiritual act by which man ceases to live unreflectively and begins to devote himself to his life with reverence in order to raise it to its true value." An illness or disability can often be the catalyst that transforms our approach to life completely. We may begin to appreciate and enjoy life as never before. We may realize the importance and value of our life, and recognize its true potential.

Celebrating life means living it fully, joyfully, and enthusiastically. It means doing all we can in a loving, peaceful way, and letting go of all the things we can't control. It means appreciating what is instead of lamenting what isn't. It means being fully present in each moment as it comes, and letting go of the past and future. Celebrating life simply means recognizing it, embracing it, and *living* it—no matter what physical conditions we may experience.

Challenged to Change—Challenged to Choose

Illness and physical impairment challenge us to let go and allow the natural flow of constant change to occur in ourselves and our lives. They challenge us to choose the attitudes and behaviors that will best facilitate our inner happiness and mental, emotional, and spiritual growth.

I'm not going to tell you that following certain practices or adopting certain attitudes will cure your illness or disability. But I will tell you that your attitudes and behaviors are *always* your own choice. Those choices determine the quality of your day-to-day life, regardless of illnesses, injuries, or disabling conditions that may occur in your body.

Aging

Leo Buscaglia writes, "The human body does not function in top form forever. This is a normal process and there is nothing wrong with it. Problems arise when we deny the process and become trapped in wishing it were otherwise." Whether or not we ever experience illness or disability in our lives, we must *all* face the realities of aging. This process presents us with the same challenges to accept changes, and to choose our attitudes and behaviors regarding those changes.

Dorothy feels the way many of us do as we grow older. "I love aging in some ways," she says. "I love being so much better at relationships, at my work, and at life in general than I was ever capable of being when I was younger. I love being past all those games and nonsense and pain that seem to be a part of youth. I love being where I am in terms of my self-confidence and internal security. But I really do hate watching and feeling my body change."

As we move through adulthood, we may feel no desire to recapture the mental, emotional, or spiritual states of our youth. We may have no interest in reliving the situations and experiences of years gone by. We may appreciate and even relish our experience, growth, and maturity. But how many of us would turn down a magic genie offering a return to the body we had when we were younger?

While a balance of healthy eating, exercise, and rest can be excellent self-care, it's also important to face and accept the challenges of change and choice as we age. Magical thinking about somehow arresting the natural aging process is self-defeating. It can only create depression, anger, and guilt over the normal changes that occur in every human body.

Cultural Pressures

Culturally, we're pretty obsessed with the physical characteristics of youth. Advertisers use young, perfectly fit models to sell their products, and often airbrush the photos to an even more unrealistic fantasy of youthful perfection. These messages are hard to misinterpret.

Just as we worship an ideal of perfect health, we idolize a mythical notion of perfect youth. Perhaps as the baby-boom generation—the largest segment of the American population—moves through middle age, we'll see changes in these attitudes. But right now, we can begin examining our cultural symbols and the myths they reflect. We can begin maturing into a more realistic viewpoint of aging, and let go of our ego's delusions of eternal youth.

We can resist cultural pressures by recognizing them as expressions of our ego's fear and resistance to change. Think about the development of a child from birth through adolescence. It would be ridiculous to choose, say ten, as the perfect age, and wish to arrest the child's development at that level. It is equally ridiculous to decide that a particular stage of adulthood, say twenty-seven, is the point at which to stop changing. The truth is, change is constant from the very beginning to the very end of our lives, even if this isn't reflected in the mass media.

Facing Physical Changes

I'm not pretending that some things are not physically easier at age twenty than forty or fifty or older. It's natural to wish for physical strength, endurance, and ease of movement. The changes in these areas that go along with aging can be frustrating and difficult, or they can just be a little annoying. It depends on our attitude of acceptance. If we insist on trying to do things we can't physically do anymore—like eating certain things, drinking alcohol, smoking, or overexertion—we're asking for trouble. We may push our bodies to the breaking point while trying to prove we are still young and fit.

But a great deal of our resistance to the changes of aging have more to do with appearance. We don't like wrinkles, gray or thinning hair, a gain or shift in our weight, or having to wear glasses. We'll do just about anything to hide or alter the physical characteristics of our age. In recent years, more and more products and treatments have been developed for this purpose. Hair transplants are commonplace, and cosmetic surgery is no longer a rare experience, limited to movie stars and accident victims.

There is nothing wrong with taking care of our appearance. It can be a healthy expression of self-esteem. But it can also become an unhealthy obsession or reaction to outside pressures. Our ego easily becomes entangled in a never-ending quest for a youthful appearance.

We may feel guilty and ashamed for losing our hair, our skin's elasticity, or the figure of our teenage years. Acceptance and a realistic perspective can free us of these self-defeating attitudes. We can let go of the things we can't control, and instead, learn to enjoy every day of our lives, whatever age we might be. We can learn to see the beauty in every stage of our body's evolution, and begin to understand the purpose for which our body exists to begin with. It is here to help us communicate with each other and to learn the lessons of life. Aging itself contains many of those important lessons.

Our Self-Image

Self-image has become a regular part of these chapters because it is fundamental to how we react to and handle all the outer conditions of our lives. If we remain stuck in a self-image that rests solely on our physical beings, we can't face the challenges of aging in a healthy, happy way. If our self-image comes from some old mental picture we had of ourselves when we were younger, we can't open up to the changes and choices of our continuing life.

Instead, we can explore our whole selves—mind, body, and spirit—discovering all our abilities and aspects, and learning to develop and use them in the best possible ways. We can view our physical aging as a normal process that can open us up to many new experiences and insights. We can put our feelings and beliefs about aging in their proper perspective.

Old Rules

Amy says, "When I was growing up, women over thirty were never supposed to wear their hair longer than chin-length. In fact, all of the women I knew wore their hair very short. It was supposed to draw the eye upwards to de-emphasize the sagging skin of the face, or something like that."

While she says such rigid fashion rules are now passé, Amy also says she worries about wearing her hair long now that she's in her thirties. "I've always liked my hair long," she says. "But I don't want to look like a middle-aged woman who's trying to look like a teenager. There are people who don't know they're not aging gracefully. I've seen them—professional women in their fifties in see-through blouses and mini-skirts. They just don't know what they look like. I worry about that."

Labels and rigid rules are usually quite useless and even harmful. We can let go of all the old rules we may have stored away in our minds about aging. We can give up our old beliefs about what each age is like before we even get there. We can examine our feelings about our bodies and getting older, our reactions to cultural pressures about youthfulness, and our self-image. When we heal our feelings and attitudes by turning to our spirit's viewpoint, we can relax into our own style of appearance without trying to look or act "old enough" or "young enough" for our age.

We Waste Our Youth

We may be taught culturally that our youth is the best time of our life. After that, we supposedly decline, do less, enjoy less, and just watch helplessly as our bodies decay and our lives narrow. But the truth is, most of us aren't very smart when our bodies are young. We haven't had the time to learn very much, or the years of experiences that help us become serene and understanding and truly happy.

Many of us spent our youth in active addiction or codependency. One woman, a recovering alcoholic, talks about her "arrested maturation process." Another says she "started going through adolescence at the age of thirty-seven" after her divorce. A man says, "I feel like I have a lot of lost time. I'm afraid that I think I'm younger than I really am."

By the time we finally work through all kinds of old stuff and start becoming able to love ourselves and others, to open ourselves to learning, growing, and contributing to the world around us, our bodies are showing the effects of more than a few years on the earth. We may feel as if we've been reborn spiritually, mentally, and emotionally, but our bodies are starting to wear out. It just doesn't seem fair.

Coming to terms with our aging process means accepting the time we may have "lost" or "wasted" along the way. We needn't attempt to recapture those lost years, and we can't, anyway. We can accept our entire past as it happened and go forward from here. We can be gentle with ourselves, accepting the realities of our own pasts. We can understand all the necessary lessons we've learned throughout our lives, even from painful or difficult experiences.

Just because we can never have the body we had at eighteen again, doesn't mean we have to be unhappy with the body we have now. We can take care of ourselves physically, emotionally, mentally, and spiritually, and enjoy greater health and fitness of mind, body, and spirit than ever before. We can live fully and happily in the present rather than longing for the past that will never come again. We can let go of the things we can't change, and accept the challenge to change what we can.

Milestones

There are certain ages that signal turning points or milestones for many of us. These may vary individually, depending on our own backgrounds and lives. The main thing to remember about these birthdays is that they can be used as wonderful opportunities to take stock—*in the present tense*—and make needed changes. We can also use them to celebrate our progress and current strengths. We can discover some things we still want to do, and start planning and working toward accomplishing those goals.

But milestone birthdays are often excuses for depression, self-pity, anger, resentment, and inaction. "It's too late now, anyway," we may whine about the things we haven't done or changes we know we need to make. We may find it painful to remember what we thought our lives would be like at certain ages when we were young. But we can mourn and release those old images.

171

Things just don't always turn out the way we expected; there are too many variables we couldn't foresee or understand when we were younger.

When we let go of our old expectations, we can move on to fully experiencing the specific joys of each new era in our lives. Sometimes we find a new sense of self-confidence or authority with a new age. Sometimes we discover that our lives are truly better than they ever have been before, and we have evolved to a healthier, happier place than we ever thought possible. Sometimes just accepting where we are right now, today, dissolves all the old blocks to peace, joy, and true self-contentment.

"You're only as old as you feel."

Age isn't meaningless, but it may not mean what our culture or family has told us it meant. We experience different things at different ages, and all of these things are valuable and important. Our aging bodies hold many lessons for us. Our evolving lives contain a continuum of growth experiences. Once we break out of our old assumptions and prejudices about aging, we can begin to really experience it fully and joyfully.

When he turned forty, Steve felt depressed. He tried sharing his feelings with his friends, but he says, "People would slap me on the back, and say 'Hey, buddy, you're only as old as you feel!' I'd smile and nod, but I'd be thinking, *I* feel *about a hundred.* I managed to pull myself together, take stock of my life, and make a lot of major changes. It was really good for me—all that painful soul searching. I just realized that I wasn't going to live forever, and it was time to start living, *really* living. So I did."

The realization that we are not going to live forever isn't a call to hedonistic pleasure seeking or self-indulgence. It's a call to wake up to our real, true inner self, our spirit, our *life*. Our bodies challenge us—through illness, disability, and aging—to make the changes and choices of *life*. When we accept the challenge, we discover what it means to live in the present, fully, joyfully, enthusiastically, and happily, with *any* physical conditions.

Exercises

Exercise One

Find the Message. If your body is ill or disabled, look for whatever you can learn from the experience. Do you need to get more rest? More exercise? Eat more healthy foods? How are you feeling emotionally? Is there anything you need to examine and resolve in this area of your life?

Exercise Two

Changes. What changes do you need to make in order to heal or adapt to your health condition? Do you feel any resistance within yourself to making these changes? Where does this resistance come from? Unrealistic expectations? Magical thinking? Perfectionism? Fear? Are you seeking and accepting the help you need?

Exercise Three

Choices. What choices are within your control right now? Do you need to make any decisions about surgery, treatments, or anything else regarding your health? Do you have all the information you need to make this decision?

Exercise Four

Accepting Your Aging Process. Examine your beliefs and attitudes about aging. What did you expect of the age you are right now? How does the reality compare to what you expected? How do you feel about that? What old rules, assumptions, or prejudices do you have about aging? Let go of the past and enjoy your current age, whatever it is. Celebrate your birthdays with joy. Pat yourself on the back for all your progress, and look forward with optimism and hope.

CHAPTER TEN

Sudden Loss and Change

*Our losses change us and change the course of our
lives. It's not that one can never again be happy
following an experience of loss. The reality is simply
that one can never again be the same.*

—Ann Kaiser Stearns

Sudden, unexpected change can create the greatest
of all challenges to our peace and serenity. With no
advance preparation, we have to adjust to what may be
drastically different circumstances than what we're used
to. We may come home from a normal day at work to
find our house has burned to the ground. We may
rejoice in a pregnancy and then have it suddenly end
in miscarriage or stillbirth. We may lose a loved one
through death or divorce. We may lose our property,
beliefs, future plans, feelings of safety, or even our sense
of identity. The truth is, almost everything in our lives
can be lost.

Most of the time we protect ourselves from this reality.
We just don't think about the fact that we could lose
something dear to us in an instant. To dwell on this
thought would make it impossible to get on with our
lives in a positive way. We don't need to fear loss or
begin grieving before anything has happened. But we
can accept the reality that it *could* happen, and that

we'd eventually come out of the experience all right if it did. This kind of rational acceptance without irrational fear can help prepare us for an unexpected loss.

Two kinds of changes take place within us when we experience a sudden loss. First, we become conscious of our vulnerability. We can no longer achieve that denial which kept us oblivious to all the things that *could* happen. We *know* that all kinds of losses can happen to us, not just to other people. We may never feel quite as safe again. The other effect of sudden loss is that eventually we adjust to it. It may take a long time, but we gradually incorporate the loss into our lives and go on.

These two changes can be very positive and healing. We needn't view acceptance of our vulnerability or of our specific loss as resignation to life's terrible aspects. Instead, we can think of this growth experience as a stepping-stone on our path toward true inner peace and rational acceptance of reality.

Disturbances in the Field

In her book, *Disturbances in the Field,* novelist Lynn Sharon Schwartz describes how a woman, her marriage, and her life are affected by the sudden deaths of two of her children. A "disturbance in the field," she explains, is something that happens outside ourselves that changes our lives. It comes along unexpectedly, and instantly, everything is different. We have to look at everything in a new way, we have to re-evaluate and readjust ourselves because of the disturbance.

There are many incidents in life that we could call "disturbances in the field." Death, divorce, the loss of a job or business, natural disasters, crimes, and car, plane, or train accidents can all create sudden major changes in our lives. For some of us, the outcome of political elections can mean drastic differences in our futures. Sudden shifts in financial matters can mean riches or ruin in that area of our lives. Life means change, and sometimes those changes happen very suddenly and unexpectedly.

Death

Joseph Campbell said, "One can experience an un-conditional affirmation of life only when one has accepted death, not as contrary to life, but as an aspect of it." It's easy to be so philosophical about death—until someone close to us dies. It's not that the view of death described above isn't a good one, or that we stop believing in it, it's just that we need to let ourselves experience our own personal loss. We can use our philosophical view as a basis for our gradual acceptance of a loved one's death, and we can eventually regain our acceptance of death in general. But when death hits close to home, we must allow ourselves to experience the grieving process.

The death of a family member or friend is one of the most common forms of loss. All of us will probably experience this kind of loss at some time in our lives. Even the death of a beloved pet can have the same kinds of effects on us. Losing a person or animal that is important to us requires a period of reacting, mourning, and ultimate acceptance. When we try to ignore or rush ourselves through these stages, we can get stuck in unresolved grief. To regain our inner peace and equilibrium, we don't suppress or deny any of our feelings or stages of grief. Instead, we allow ourselves to grow through them.

Depending on who has died, we may require a wide range of time to fully recover. This doesn't mean that we can't do anything else during this time, or that we must drape ourselves in black and cry all the time for a specified period. It just means that we can expect to feel the stages of grief, perhaps intermittently, over a period of time. We can expect some sad days and some better days, some fearful, lonely, angry, and peaceful days. Eventually, we *can* recover a balance of happiness and joy in life. But until then, it's okay to feel up and down for a while.

Sometimes other people can be a tremendous help to us at these times. But sometimes, even with the best intentions, other people can be more of an additional burden than a help. Many of us simply don't know what to do for people who are mourning. Their feelings may make us uncomfortable, and we may not want to let them express those feelings. We may try to answer their questions, such as *why* this death has occurred, rather than simply letting them express their grief in their own way. Rabbi Harold Kushner writes, "We help the person who asks 'why?' not by explaining *why,* but by easing his pain, validating his right to cry and feel angry, and telling him that we care about him."

When Gillian's husband died in a plane crash, she says everyone seemed to want to treat her like a child. "They kept trying to take over everything," she says. "They started going through our business papers to find the insurance policies and things like that. They called the funeral home and made all the arrangements. They kept trying to take my children away and drug me up. It was so stupid. What did they *expect* me to feel and to do? My husband had been killed with no warning. I just wanted to hold my babies and cry for a while. What was wrong with that? I could have handled all the business that needed taking care of too. But everyone kept trying to tell me what to do. Why couldn't they just *ask* me what I needed them to do?"

Openly expressed grief may make us feel quite uncomfortable. What should we do? How should we respond? What kind of help is appropriate? This is largely an individual matter, but it's safe to say that grieving persons need to be allowed to grieve. They also need to be respected and not treated as if they've lost their minds. It doesn't take much to see that running errands, shopping for food, making coffee, and cleaning up probably won't step on anyone's toes, but a bereaved spouse, parent, or adult child should be consulted about any business matters that need attending to.

As Harold Kushner wrote, it's not our place to tell a grieving person *why* a tragedy has occurred, but just to hold the person's hand, let him or her know that we're nearby and we care. Maybe we understand how the person feels, and maybe we don't. Assumptions and explanations aren't helpful. Stories of other tragedies aren't helpful. Sharing a hug or a cup of coffee are sometimes the best offerings of help we can give.

Whether it's the death of a friend, spouse, child, parent, lover, or pet, death requires us to adjust to a permanent change in our lives. This may be one of the most difficult changes we have to accept in life, but it can be done, given time and understanding. We can go on with our lives without those we may have thought we'd have with us forever. We can accept the necessary changes in our lives and ourselves. We can recover and continue to live our lives, well and even happily—but differently.

179

We can eventually accept death philosophically, as a part of life. We can use our faith in a Higher Power or the eternal life of our spirit to help us accept the death of the body. We can examine our beliefs pragmatically, and let go of any that make us fearful or unable to grow through our grieving process. We can embrace those beliefs that help us accept the reality of death, and move on to living a changed but full, peaceful, happy life.

Divorce

The end of a marriage or long-term love relationship can require the same grief process as coming to terms with a death. Even if the relationship was unhappy for a long time, adjusting to the changes divorce brings can be a long, difficult process. We may go through all the same stages of denial, depression, guilt, anger, fear, and acceptance.

Some of the changes necessary after separating from our spouse involve things like living alone, doing all those domestic things like shopping, cooking, cleaning, and paying the bills by ourselves. There are changes in our social life, our circle of friends and family, and our habits of entertainment. There are changes in our self-image and our public image—we are no longer part of a couple.

All of these changes, and many more, will have to be faced and resolved eventually. But the inner process of grieving for the lost relationship is often done with less understanding and help from other people. Well-meaning friends may try to cheer us up or get us out into socializing and dating before we feel ready. We may feel foolish or ashamed for feeling all the feelings of grief over an ended relationship. We may hide or repress our true feelings, only prolonging the grief recovery process.

Likening our loss to the death of a loved one may help us to understand and accept our own grief process. Even if our marriage was very unhappy for us, it was an important part of our lives, and we need to let go of it through the gradual process of grieving. We can easily get stuck in one of the stages of grief if we don't look at the situation from a new, realistic viewpoint, and let ourselves grow through the process.

Recovery from an ended relationship doesn't happen overnight, or by quickly finding someone else to attach ourselves to. It happens slowly, stage by stage, with time and effort. We may have a lot of old hurt, anger, and sadness to work through. We may have "lost years" to let go of before we can begin moving forward. Whatever our own circumstances, we have to turn to a new way of looking at things. A relationship has ended, and that part of our lives will never again be the same. We are shaken out of our old viewpoint and it is up to us to choose our new one. It is entirely within our power to choose a more positive one.

"Acts of God"

Natural disasters such as earthquakes, fires, tornados, hurricanes, volcanos, electrical storms, droughts, floods, mud slides, and snowstorms can affect many of us suddenly and dramatically. These "acts of God" can leave us injured or homeless in a matter of minutes. They can ruin our crops, take away our livelihood, and destroy all kinds of property. Insurance money, when it's available, may provide little consolation for such emotion-packed losses.

There is no one to blame for these natural occurrences—except God. And often, God does get blamed. We feel angry and victimized by fate or chance. We wonder why our house was destroyed while our neighbor's stands untouched. We may resent the banker whose job continues, while we must give up our family farm. We may find all kinds of ways to blame, blame, blame.

The truth is, these things happen. They can happen anytime, anywhere. No one is entirely safe from the earth's natural phenomena. But blame is a part of the grieving process, and as long as we recognize this and let ourselves grow past it, we can recover from any loss. We can let ourselves grow through the grief process and find ways to look at the situation positively. We can discover new wonders in ourselves and the world when we let go of clinging to our old views.

Natural disasters don't happen because we deserve some kind of punishment. They're nature's normal behavior. They happen because it is natural for them to happen. Unfortunately, we are sometimes in the way and consequently get hurt, either by the actual occurrence or its results. In any case, we can accept them and our own resulting grief process. As in all the other cases of sudden loss, we can look at things in a new way, discover positive options, and make new choices that will lead us to our best possible futures. We truly *can* recover from anything.

The Grief Process

When faced with a sudden loss, most of us react strongly with denial, fear, anger, guilt, sadness, confusion, and perhaps a sense of numbness. Our body and mind provide all kinds of cushions to help us take in the news and assimilate it slowly. Before we can adjust to the change, we need some time just to absorb its reality.

The word *trauma* is defined as an emotional experience or shock that has lasting psychic effects. Sudden loss is shocking and emotional and can't help but have lasting effects on our minds and hearts. The physical equivalent to an emotional trauma is a violent wound to the body. We can think of this as a metaphor for emotional trauma or sudden loss. A wound is inflicted, suddenly and violently; it is felt deeply; it is then recognized for what it is, treated accordingly, and begins to heal. It hurts as it heals, growing stronger and more whole all the while. Eventually, the pain eases and it is restored to health and wholeness. But scar tissue remains, manifesting permanent change. Sometimes, as in the case of a broken bone, the mended place is stronger than it ever was before.

It is important to accept and allow ourselves to react initially to sudden loss. We can't skip over any of the stages necessary for recovery from loss any more than we can skip ahead to healed skin or bones. We must go through a healing process, which may start out quite painfully and take a very long time to complete. Eventually, we may become stronger than we ever were before. But we can only begin recovering our peace and serenity by first allowing ourselves to go through the initial stages of reaction to our loss.

Denial

When his cousin died, Charlie seemed to react calmly. He and his cousin had been close, and her death was sudden and violent. But Charlie went through the days following her death in a normal, rational frame of mind.

He seemed to "take it very well," everyone said. He helped make funeral arrangements, picked up family friends at the airport, made phone calls, and ran errands for everyone. He was even able to talk about his cousin without showing any emotion.

After the funeral, Charlie returned to his normal activities. He began having nightmares, which would wake him up in the middle of the night, but he'd forget them as soon as he woke up. Finally, several months after his cousin's death, he woke up from a nightmare, sobbing her name. He cried all night, in his wife's arms. After that night, Charlie felt depressed off and on for months, gradually coming to accept his cousin's death on a conscious level.

Our first reaction to the death of a loved one is often this kind of numb denial. Especially for men, showing our true emotions may be difficult. It may be hard to even know what true emotions are. The initial stages of reaction to death are often marked by apparent calm. Sometimes, it may seem as if we simply refuse to believe what's happened. We may talk about the deceased person as if he or she were still alive. We may forget not to set a place for the person at the table.

We may react with this same denial and confusion to all kinds of sudden loss, whether it's loss of property, money, a relationship, a job, or a cherished belief. We just don't quite believe it at first. There is a period of transition when we may hold contradicting realities in our minds. The old hasn't quite given way to the new yet.

While our spirits always accept change with love and peacefulness, that doesn't mean that the feelings and reactions of our ego are bad or wrong. At this stage, it's important to remember to be gentle with ourselves and allow ourselves to grow through the grief process. What we're feeling is normal for a person in our situation to be feeling, and we can let ourselves feel it until we don't need to anymore. We *will* come out of this stage eventually.

Depression

After we have passed through the initial period of denial, we often become depressed. We begin letting ourselves feel the sadness, and perhaps even despair, of facing our new loss. We may feel hopeless, helpless, and powerless. We may feel unable to do more than go through the motions of our daily lives. We may spend many months feeling as if we're living in a fog of sorrow.

In her book, *Living Through Personal Crisis,* Ann Kaiser Stearns writes, "For most people, depression is the main feature of grieving and it involves the longest struggle." We may feel at times as if there is no point to going on. We may feel that our loss has overwhelmed us, and we'll never recover from it. But the truth is that we are experiencing the normal and necessary stages of grief.

We *will* come through this stage too. We just need to remember that what we're going through takes time. We can gently accept ourselves and our need to mourn our loss. We can remember to make an effort to keep active, accept help from others, and not beat ourselves up for being human. We can let ourselves grow through the process by simply accepting it.

Guilt

As we gradually accept the reality of our loss, we may begin looking for ways in which we contributed to it. We may become obsessed with self-blame and guilt. For example, if we have a miscarriage, stillbirth, or unhealthy child, we may go over and over in our minds everything we thought, felt, ate, drank, did, and didn't do while pregnant. A husband may blame himself for any secretly negative feelings he may have had about the pregnancy.

We may feel unable for a while to stop our minds from a constant barrage of "If only . . ." thoughts: *If only I hadn't let her go out tonight, she wouldn't have been in the car accident. . . . If only I had sold the farm before the drought, we'd have plenty of money now. . . . If only I'd had a baby, my marriage wouldn't have ended.*

Whatever the kind of loss, we may think of a million ways in which we caused it or could have prevented it. These thoughts, while not necessarily true or rational, are a sign that we are growing through our grief. We are trying to make sense of things. We are beginning to accept what's happened. We may imagine all kinds of scenarios depicting how things could have been different, but this is the beginning of facing what actually has happened. Again, we can gently accept our need to go through this stage of mourning our loss, and remember that, eventually, our ego will let go and our spirit will show us another viewpoint.

Anger

Another stage we commonly go through in the grief process is blaming others. When her grandfather died while in the hospital for a routine repair of a slipped disc, Janis was outraged. "I wanted to sue the doctors, the hospital, and anyone else I could," she says. "My grandfather had no heart disease or anything like that—there was no *reason* why he should have had a heart attack. He was old, but he was healthy otherwise. The doctors and nurses *must* have been to blame."

Whether or not anyone's negligence or treatment of her grandfather contributed to his death, Janis was angry because he died. Sometimes we blame medical personnel, other family members, friends, strangers, or even God for our losses. While our anger may seem justified in many cases, it doesn't undo the loss or help us feel better. But we sometimes need to go through a period of anger as part of our healing process.

Sometimes this anger is directed at the deceased person. We feel angry at being left, abandoned by the person who is no longer living. We may feel cheated out of time we thought we'd have together, or help we thought the other person would be there to give us. We may resent all the time we feel was wasted in the past. If only we'd known, we may think, we would have conducted our relationship differently. Now we'll never get that chance.

These issues can be resolved in our own minds and hearts, even though we can never resolve them face-to-face with the deceased person. We can learn to forgive ourselves, others, and life for being the way it is. We can use our newfound understanding of the vulnerability we all share to improve our other and future relationships. We can thank the person who's died for the time we shared, and let them go.

When faced with losses other than death, we may have more opportunities for resolution of our angry feelings. We may be able to see the remorse in someone who has caused us harm. They may be able to make amends in some way. We may outgrow our feelings that the loss is the permanent end of something important to us. We may begin to see that it is merely a change to which we can adapt and through which we may even improve ourselves and our lives.

Even when another person is clearly responsible for our loss, we can learn to forgive them and go on with our lives. Carrying anger and hatred within us only poisons ourselves and condemns us to misery. Gradually, we can learn to let go of our anger and to forgive others and ourselves. With time and understanding, we can grow through this experience toward even greater love and inner peace than we ever thought possible.

Fear

Now that we have gone through the stages of denial, depression, guilt, and anger, we may begin to realize that *things will never be quite the same again*. This realization may fill us with apprehension and fear. We may feel a sense of vulnerability and powerlessness. We are beginning to face our future, changed as it now must be.

We can be gentle with ourselves as we move through this stage of recovery. We can accept our need to face the future wondering what we'll do now, how things will be for us, who will be there with us. Change requires this examination, and fear may accompany our initial look at a future we hadn't planned on. We can understand this fear and not just survive it, but grow through it.

We know that fear is of our ego, since our spirit is always fearless. But we may need some time to feel our ego's fear before we can turn to our spirit's viewpoint. We may need some time to look at our new circumstances or situation as our ego always looks at the unfamiliar—fearfully. Then we can move through our fear to a new acceptance of whatever changes we face.

If we understand our ego's fearfulness, we can move through this stage more peacefully. We can accept that we need to get through the fear in order to come out on the other side—the side of acceptance.

Acceptance

The final stage of grief is acceptance. This doesn't mean we will never again miss the person we've lost, or that we won't ever experience longing for the old days, before things changed in some particular way. It means we have fully experienced and grown through all the stages of grieving for our loss. It means we can get on with our lives in a new way.

We reorder our perspective and reorganize our thoughts, beliefs, and lives to accommodate our loss. We have allowed ourselves to feel all the feelings of grief and are ready to feel new feelings and experience new things. There may be some residual feelings from time to time, feelings we thought we had already worked through, but that's okay. Some things in ourselves and our lives will return to normal, others will never be the same again.

It may be a very long time before we can see all we've learned from this experience. We may have been transformed in wonderfully positive ways that will serve us in the future. But for now, we can simply accept that the worst is over and we have regained our equilibrium. We have accepted the reality of our loss and begun to move on in new ways. We are beginning to be able to see new possibilities opening up for us. We are incorporating hope and love and peace into our new viewpoint. We are recovering—not returning to our past, but moving on to our future.

Growing Through the Process

While the stages of grief described above pertain to all kinds of loss, there are some differences in how and how long we may need to recover from different types of losses. It may take a few weeks to move through the stages of grief over the loss of a job or promotion, while a year or longer may be needed to fully recover from the loss of a loved one. We may feel we're going along just fine until something suddenly reminds us of our loss, and old feelings are rekindled. All of these variations are normal, and we can accept them as part of the process instead of thinking we *should* be over something by now, or we *shouldn't* feel a certain way anymore. We can accept our own growth patterns and experiences as they happen, and know we are going to be all right.

Sudden loss or change can be a tremendous opportunity for learning. We can stretch our minds and hearts in new ways we never imagined before. We can gain insight and strength from the necessary re-evaluation process that recovery provides. We can discover a new outlook on life, other people, and ourselves that can improve our future.

A new self-image may emerge from all the growing we do in recovery. We may realize potential strengths and abilities we never knew we had. We may begin to accept the vulnerability of being human, knowing that we will be all right no matter what happens. We may grow in matters of trust, faith, and love for ourselves and others. We may begin to know ourselves as never before.

Time is said to heal all wounds. But we know that we must use our recovery time in positive, loving ways. We must help ourselves and allow others to help us.

We must look at things in a new way. Healing is a matter of time, faith, hope, and effort. We can make it easier on ourselves, and greater in its ultimate rewards. Spiritual equanimity can enter into our minds and hearts, if we let it. This is not the belief that we are invincible in the physical sense, but invincible in the sense that we will be all right no matter what happens in the outer world. Accidents *will* happen. Recovery to new heights of peace, love, and well-being can happen too. Loving ourselves through the process is all we need to do.

Exercises

Exercise One

The Grief Process. Review the stages of grief in this chapter. See if you can apply them to any loss in your life. It can be a small change or a large one. See how the stages can be applied to a wide variety of situations, relationships, and circumstances. Accept your need to go through the stages without hurry or impatience.

Exercise Two

Remembering Crises. Think back to another time in your life. Go back far enough to look at a crisis objectively. Now list all the *positive* results of this experience. What did you learn? How did you grow? How have you been able to use the lessons of this experience in other cases? What talents, abilities, or strengths did you discover in yourself? How have the resulting changes this experience brought helped you to become stronger?

CHAPTER ELEVEN

Atmospheres

We tend to take on the coloration of the setting in which we find ourselves.

—Harold Kushner

The atmospheres in which we live may be one of the most important and overlooked conditions of our lives. We may disregard or underestimate the influence of our surroundings on our feelings, moods, and outlook. Or we may underestimate our ability to change and control our environments. We may feel anxious, angry, or depressed about conditions over which we have no control, while doing little to exercise the real choices we have in this area.

We usually can't control the decor of the offices where we work, or the stores where we shop. We can't change the view from a window, or the sounds of trains, planes, or cars nearby. Many of us can't afford to renovate our homes, or buy ones with all of the specific atmospheric conditions we want. Accepting the things we can't change is necessary for our peace and happiness, but we can probably all do more than we're doing to enhance our environment.

Where are you right now? What are your surroundings? What sounds, smells, and sights do you perceive? How do they make you feel? Are they pleasant? Irritating?

Orderly? Beautiful? Can you really concentrate peacefully on what you're reading? What changes can you make right now to enhance your environment? Turn off the radio? Open or close a window? Tidy up your desk or room? Feed the dog so he stops barking? We don't have to spend money or turn everything upside down to start making small, positive changes.

We really are affected by the surroundings in which we try to work, play, eat, read, socialize, rest, relax, and live. We may respond with tension, anxiety, nervousness, or even anger to certain environments. But most of us just feel irritated or complain about our surroundings without trying to make them peaceful. We can all make some changes to our surroundings to help us feel better in them.

In her book, *Beyond Codependency,* Melody Beattie describes how she grew from hating her run-down home to transforming it into a beautiful haven for herself and her family—and did it with very little money. She writes, "I worked and worked, and I had three floors of beautiful home. . . . I learned how to make something out of almost nothing, instead of nothing out of something." We make nothing out of something when we give in to our ego's negative reactions to the things in our environments that we can change. Instead, let's concentrate on the something that is within our reach.

The Pragmatic Approach

Wherever we are, we can begin examining the things we can change. We can ask ourselves the two key questions we have used before: *Is it harmful?* and, *Is it helpful?* Then we can begin eliminating negatives and creating positives in our environments. As William George Jordan wrote in *The Majesty of Calmness,* "In justice to ourselves we should refuse to live in an atmosphere that keeps us from living our best."

For example, we may be in the habit of turning on the television or radio as soon as we wake up in the morning and keeping it on until we leave the house. We can ask ourselves if this habit might be contributing to some of the irritation, hurriedness, or distracted feeling we have at that time of day. We may be making it impossible to hear the birds chirping, or even our families trying to talk to us. We may be starting out our day in a more noisy, frenzied way than we'd really like.

If we find negative effects of any habit or element of our environment, we can begin to eliminate or change it in positive ways. We might try a week without the TV or radio in the morning, and just see what happens. We may discover a peaceful silence or lovely nature sounds or a calm, loving time to spend with our family. If we live in a particularly noisy place, we may prefer to use some tapes or records of beautiful, peaceful music or nature sounds, rather than the chatter of TV or radio to mask the noise.

Taking a pragmatic approach simply means discovering the things that we can do to enhance our own surroundings. It means becoming sensitive to how we react to sounds, smells, and sights around us. It means opening our minds to the possibilities of a more peaceful, happy environment within our reach. This kind of self-examination takes a little time and effort. We need to really tune in to our inner feelings and responses. We need to discover how we are affected by the things in our environments. We need to decide whether we can accept the things we can't change, remove ourselves from the place, or make positive changes.

Aren't we worth this amount of effort? Aren't our peace and happiness worth doing all we can to enhance them? As William George Jordan wrote, "We carry our house plants from one window to another to give them the proper heat, light, air, and moisture. Should we not be at least as careful of ourselves?"

Healing Environments

When visiting someone in the hospital, Harry says he remembers walking down a long corridor, past many other patients' rooms. He explains, "As I passed the doors to these rooms, I could hear the sounds of gunshots, sirens, screaming, crying, angry voices, screeching car tires, and music which was loud, exciting, dramatic and menacing, all coming from the televisions in the rooms. I remember thinking, *This is a healing environment?* When Harry asked a nurse about it, she shrugged and said, 'It's a free country. We can't tell people what they can watch on TV.' "

I'm a great believer in common sense. Do you think these things are conducive to healing? Do we really need rules and regulations to tell us we need peace, calm, beauty, joy, and rest when we're sick? Most hospitals make great efforts to provide pleasant, comfortable surroundings for their patients, but we can contribute to those efforts by our own choices.

We can turn off the television or watch only positive, uplifting programs. We can surround ourselves with photos of our loved ones, plants and flowers, stuffed animals, pictures of places we love or beautiful landscapes, beaches, or mountains. We can bring a tape player with tapes of our favorite music or nature sounds. We can read books and magazines that inspire and uplift us, or distract us with positive humor. Whether at home or in a hospital setting, there are many ways in which we can create a more peaceful, happy, loving, and healing environment for ourselves and our loved ones.

Healing does not occur only in our bodies. When we need to heal mentally, emotionally, and spiritually, we can help ourselves by choosing peaceful, loving, healing environments. We can sit in a park or on a beach, drive through the countryside, or wander through a museum or art gallery. We can find the places where we feel good and spend the time we need to there.

We can also take care to avoid places where we seem to feel unhappy. We don't have to frequent places where we tend to feel angry, sad, fearful, or depressed. As Ann Kaiser Stearns writes, "It is a self-destructive act on your part to place yourself repeatedly in settings that are alien to healing." When we need to heal in any way, we have the power to choose or create healing places for ourselves.

Sounds

We don't have to be sick to respond positively to pleasant sounds and negatively to unpleasant sounds. Eliminating disturbing noise from our environment can be as simple as turning the television, radio, or stereo down or off. It can mean making a choice between fresh air and open windows, or quiet and closed windows. In many cases, there are noises over which we have no control. We can learn to accept these calmly or, if possible, we can choose not to live, work, or play in the areas where they exist.

Everything we hear does make a difference, even if we think we're not really listening. Have you ever heard a song on the radio first thing in the morning and found yourself humming it all day—even if you don't like it?

197

The Suzuki Method of musical training makes use of this phenomenon with daily listening to tapes of great masters playing great masterpieces. The students develop an ear for classical music played correctly by repeated listening.

This is a positive way to use our mind's ability to record what it hears. But we must also take care not to allow our minds to record a lot of negative noise. This is simply a matter of learning to pay attention to what's going into our ears, and making conscious choices about what we do have control over. And that means avoiding unpleasant noise and allowing our minds the rest and clarity that we need for our inner peace and true happiness.

Music

Music has been used to help patients relax in many settings, including surgery, dentistry, and a variety of medical treatments and procedures. It is used in hospital newborn nurseries, as well as in stores, offices, and restaurants. It can make us feel cheerful, sad, hungry, tired, energized, or calm. It can help bring our deep inner feelings to the surface to be released.

Music is a very subjective experience. We each have to become sensitive to our own reactions to different kinds of music. Many people find themselves reacting very strongly to certain types of music or even to specific pieces of music. As we learn about our reactions, we can begin to eliminate music we find annoying or unpleasant in some way, and fill our environment with music that has a more positive effect on us.

Usually, our taste in music is a habit developed early in life by the kinds of music we were exposed to and the tastes of our parents, teachers, and friends. But as adults, we can learn to let go of these old biases and experiment with new forms of music. We can open our minds and explore all kinds of music we may never have thought we'd like. We can form new habits and develop new tastes based on what makes us feel good, rather than what others say we should like.

All we have to do is open our minds, and give ourselves a chance to develop new habits and tastes by repeated listening to music we find soothing, pleasant, and peaceful.

The Sounds of Nature

The sounds in our environments also include those not made by human art. Waves crashing or gently lapping on a shore; birds, whales, or wolves singing; geese honking or loons cooing—these are the sounds of nature. When we eliminate all the artificial sounds of humanity, we can hear another song humming throughout all of life. These sounds can often have a very soothing effect on us.

The gurgling of babies, the purring of kittens, the gentle sounds of birds, animals, leaves rustling, or water flowing can all make us feel good. We can find these sounds in nature around us, go to places where they can be heard, or listen to tape recordings of them. The main thing is to simply relax and hear them. In order to do this, we have to let go of all the noises and internal chatter covering them up.

Many people enjoy tapes of ocean waves or falling rain. Other people might prefer nature sounds mixed with gentle music. These kinds of tapes can be found just about anywhere tapes are sold now, but you can also make your own. Take a tape recorder out to a nature preserve or public park; a beach, river, stream, or waterfall; the bird house at your local zoo; or any-place where the sounds of nature can be heard.

Nature tapes and records can also be found at many public libraries. You can listen to them free of charge and choose the kinds of sounds to which you respond the most positively. Then you can buy or make tapes of the ones you like best. It doesn't matter where you live or how much money you have—nature is here for *all* of us. But we have to make the effort to get out there and enjoy it, or bring it into our environments through tapes.

Silence

Most of us spend very little time, if any, in total silence. We live our lives accompanied by the sounds of radio, television, cars, trucks, planes, voices, and all kinds of other noise. Even if we eliminate unnecessary noise from our environments and take care to listen to pleasant, soothing music and sounds, occasional silence can still be essential to our peace and happiness.

Silence can be a wonderful rest from constant, fren-zied thinking and being bombarded with stimulating sounds in our environments. Silence can relax us physi-cally, mentally, and emotionally. It can give us the chance to tune in to ourselves and reconnect with our inner peace and Higher Power. It is often in silence that we discover our spirit.

We can create a time and place for silence every day. It doesn't need to be more than a few minutes, as long as we really allow ourselves to let go of mental chatter and experience the silence fully. It can be done first thing in the morning, last thing at night, or both. It can be done on our coffee break at work, while our children are napping, or between classes. We can do it in a bathroom, bedroom, car, library, museum, or chapel.

Silence is indeed golden. It can provide us with the riches of peace, calm, tranquility, balance, and awareness of our spirituality. We can return from it rested, refreshed, and ready to face all the conditions of our lives with equanimity. It can be the well from which we draw the strength of peacefulness. And it's available to all of us at some time in every day. It's up to us to use it.

Sights

The things we see around us can be pleasant, irritating, ugly, beautiful, soft, hard, exciting, or calming. They can be depressing, uplifting, inspiring, touching, or fear provoking. We may not always be aware of the effects these sights are having on our moods, thoughts, and feelings. We may just sense that we don't like a certain place or building without really knowing why. We may feel depressed, excited, agitated, or peaceful when we are surrounded by certain colors, or by cluttered, empty, or natural places.

In *The Power of Myth,* Joseph Campbell asked, "Where is your bliss station?" We all need at least one place that feels beautiful, peaceful, safe, happy, and special to us. Some of us may have a favorite spot in a public park or out in the country. We may love certain buildings, such as historical landmarks, museums, churches, or our own homes. There may be a garden, beach, or forest where we always feel wonderful. These places are important for us to spend time alone, just *being*—getting to know ourselves and reconnecting with our spiritual self.

Joseph Campbell said, "You must have a room, or a certain hour or so a day, where you don't know what was in the newspapers that morning, you don't know who your friends are, you don't know what you owe anybody or what anybody owes you. This is a place where you can simply experience what you are and what you might be. This is the place of creative incubation. At first you may find that nothing happens there. But if you have a sacred place and use it, something eventually will happen."

In our modern world, we don't seem to have many places that feel "sacred" to us. The cathedral is no longer the central focus of our towns or lives. But we can create special places for ourselves, and, to paraphrase Joseph Campbell, we can sanctify our own landscapes, claim our environments, and make them "places of spiritual relevance" for us. We can find and create our own "bliss stations."

Green Spaces

We can't control much of what we see when we go out into the world. But we do choose many of the places where we spend our time. For example, if we feel we must remain in a job where the surroundings feel unpleasant to us, we can take walks outdoors on our breaks and lunch hour. Or, if we have time and transportation, we can go to a park, zoo, conservatory, arboretum, or other pleasant, natural place for a short while. We can leave a few minutes earlier in the morning to take the "scenic route" to work, avoiding traffic and giving ourselves a pleasant start to the day.

The human need for a little time and space with nature is important. Joseph Campbell said that a "sense of the presence of nature is a basic mood of man. But now we live in a city. It's all stone and rock, manufactured by human hands. It's a different kind of world to grow up in when you're out in the forest with the little chipmunks and the great owls. All these things are around you as presences, representing forces and powers and magical possibilities of life that are not yours and yet are all part of life, that opens it out to you. Then you find it echoing in yourself, because you are nature."

City planners deliberately create green spaces in our urban areas to give us pleasant breaks from buildings and concrete pavement. We need these spaces for the oxygen from the greenery, but also for visual rest and calm amid the city environment. We need to be around nature because we are part of it. We can take advantage of these spaces, using them for their designated purposes. We can also remember to plan our own environments as carefully.

It doesn't take a lot of space or money to create peaceful, natural places within our home environments. A little corner, room, balcony, porch, window box, deck, or backyard filled with greenery can provide a wonderful retreat. We can grow plants, trees, flowers, and vegetables, even indoors. We can learn about caring for living things and spend some of our time surrounded by beautiful greenery.

Light

We respond to the amount of light in our environments in terms of both mood and alertness. Dim lighting may tend to make us feel tired, drowsy, or bored. It may also contribute to feelings of sadness, anxiety, and hostility. Some people who are very sensitive to the changing amount of sunlight throughout the year suffer from seasonal depression. Even those of us who love rainy days need some sunlight to pick us up after a while.

Light is something we can easily control in our homes by using florescent and incandescent lighting in arrangements we find pleasant. We can experiment with different levels of brightness, color tints, and placement of our lighting fixtures. We can take care in choosing our draperies, blinds, and shades, and the times and amounts of sunlight coming into our homes from outside.

We can also remember to get outdoors frequently for a dose of natural light. Even on cloudy days there is some natural light coming through. We can learn to become aware of the effects of lighting on our moods and feelings, and begin to make some changes to get the light we need. We can also take care not to go overboard and spend long periods of time in bright, direct sunshine. This can make us feel tired and overheated. Balance is our goal in determining what kind and how much light we need.

We can analyze our reactions to lighting pragmatically. How do we feel after an afternoon in a dark conference room? After hours in bright sunshine? After shorter periods in filtered sunshine, incandescent, or florescent lighting? We can use this information to decide the best balance of light for us.

Color

In choosing the colors for our clothes, walls, cars, houses, gardens, and other elements of our environments, we can again take a pragmatic approach. What colors do we like? We can examine any reasons we wear or buy things in certain colors, such as being told by someone else that we look good in it or that it's the "in" color this year. We can begin asking ourselves what effects certain colors have on us. What pieces of clothing do we love to wear? What are our favorite buildings,

Atmospheres

rooms, and objects? What color are they? We can look around wherever we go for colors we find pleasant and attractive and fill our own personal environments with the colors we respond to most positively.

Decorators choose colors according to the mood or feeling they want to convey in a certain area. For example, we wouldn't paint a room bright red if we wanted to use the room primarily for resting—red is a stimulating color. Generally, light, soft colors are more pleasant and peaceful than bright or dark colors. There are many psychological and metaphysical theories about the effects color can have on people. If you find such things helpful, use them. But I think a simple, pragmatic approach can be an effective way for all of us to choose colors that contribute to our inner peace and happiness.

Order

Another element of our visual environment is the amount of clutter and disarray in which we find ourselves. In accumulating the things we want to have and use, we may end up with so much stuff around that our environment feels overcrowded. We may need to go through all our things and decide whether we really want to keep all of it. We may want to try organizing our things and keeping them put away in cabinets and closets to keep a clearer space in which to live.

Simplicity is generally more pleasant for human beings to deal with. Overstimulation caused by too many things clamoring for our attention is stressful. We can follow Henry David Thoreau's advice to "Simplify! Simplify!" and create a more calm, peaceful visual environment for ourselves. Cleanliness, order, and clear, open spaces can be much more pleasant and conducive to inner peace and happiness than all the modern gadgets we tend to accumulate.

Order is natural in the universe, and perhaps this is why people respond positively to it. A sense of calm, satisfaction, and peacefulness can be the effect of simple order in our environment. Uncomplicating our visual surroundings can have a very calming effect on us—even if we think of ourselves as basically sloppy people. This does not mean that we should become obsessively tidy and meticulous about order and cleanliness. But we can find ways to eliminate unnecessary clutter and simplify the effort required to maintain a calm, peaceful, orderly environment.

Beauty

Henry David Thoreau wrote, "The perception of beauty is a moral test." If we perceive beauty all around us, we are awakening the beauty within ourselves. When we can see nothing but pain, misery, and bleakness, it doesn't mean there is no beauty inside us—it means we have lost touch with that beauty. When we rediscover the beauty within ourselves, we can see beauty all around us.

We can perceive beauty in many things and places if we only open our minds to its presence and take the time to look for it. We can also deliberately go to places we find beautiful and create beauty in our environments. We can visit art galleries and museums, and fill our environments with beautiful books, paintings, fabrics, photographs, and plants or flowers.

After Hilary's surgery, she spent several days recuperating on her living room sofa. "It was the most comfortable place to rest, and I could watch TV if I wanted to," she explains. "But I found that I didn't want to. I didn't feel like reading or doing anything at all for the first few days. I remember just lying there, moving my eyes around the room, looking at everything. Having the flowers my husband brought me to look at was the most wonderful thing. My eyes kept resting on them as I laid there, and I felt this incredible appreciation for their beauty. It was a breathtaking experience."

Hilary says she used to think giving people flowers was just a social cliche, just something you were supposed to do. "But I don't feel that way anymore," she says. "I give flowers to people all the time now, and I always keep some on my desk. I'll never again underestimate the value of beauty. It made me feel wonderful."

Visual beauty can indeed make us feel wonderful. It doesn't take a lot of money either. An empty room, carefully painted, can be a beautiful space and a joy to be in. A few flower seeds can grow a garden full of gorgeous, colorful blossoms. Many cities have free or low-cost admission to museums full of artworks, furniture, and other beautiful items to view. Don't underestimate the impact just looking at beautiful things can have on your moods, feelings, and outlook.

Nature provides many beautiful visual experiences for us. Lakes, oceans, rivers, streams, trees, mountains, islands, birds, butterflies, tropical fish, coral, and many more visual feasts are available to all of us no matter where we live. We can see these things in our own area, or at museums, in books, magazines, television programs, or films. We can buy inexpensive posters of natural wonders or master artworks. There are many ways we can all surround ourselves with beauty. The first and most important step is opening our hearts and minds to it.

Scents

Our sense of smell plays an important part in our experience of any environment. Some things smell bad to us because of our body's natural aversion to harmful substances, such as spoiled food. Other reactions to scents come from our memories, both conscious and unconscious. For example, if we become ill from eating a certain food, the odor of that food can make us feel ill whenever we smell it, even if we don't remember the original incident.

Conversely, specific scents may be associated in our minds with pleasant memories, and evoke a more positive reaction. The perfume worn by someone we love, our favorite childhood foods, or even a musty attic that we used as a playroom, can all create pleasant scent-memories. One woman says the fumes of city buses remind her of the happy, exciting trips she took as a child growing up on a farm. Any scent that reminds us of a pleasant event or person in our lives can smell good to us.

There do seem to be some scents that we find universally appealing. Many people like the smells of freshly cut grass, rain, bread baking, hot apple pie, cinnamon and other spices, flowers, herbs, and fresh fruits. The human brain seems to react with relaxation, pleasure, alertness, and many other positive feelings to such scents. Manufacturers take great care to produce household products we will buy because we like the way they smell.

We can fill our lives with the scents we like best. Selecting soaps and other scented products carefully can help keep us surrounded by scents we enjoy. We can open our windows for fresh air periodically, or hang our wash outside rather than using a dryer. We can use candles, scented oils, or simmer cinnamon and other spices in water on the stove to fill our home with a pleasant scent.

Other People

William George Jordan wrote, "Every man has an atmosphere which is affecting every other." We've all been around people who seemed to bring out the worst in us. They may trigger our fears, anger, worry, anxiety, or negative expectations and reactions. They may carry with them attitudes and behaviors that set off our egos in all kinds of unpleasant ways. Everyone *does* have an atmosphere about them that affects others.

It's hard to respect ourselves when we spend a lot of time around people who don't respect us. Certain people and circumstances can appeal strongly to our egos, and embroil us in destructive ego games. It's okay to avoid this by avoiding these people. We all know how others sometimes damage our peace and tranquility. We all know how the atmosphere in our home can change by the presence of a houseguest. The delicate balance of relationships and self-images changes.

Donna says she feels very different whenever her husband's brother comes to visit. "He used to be around a lot more often, and I thought nothing was ever really different when he was with us," she says. "But now, time has gone by and I guess we've changed. When he's around now, *everything's* different. I can feel myself acting differently, talking differently, even sitting and moving differently. I feel my body language protecting myself. My husband acts differently too, and we act differently toward each other. It's almost as if it's not *us* when my brother-in-law is around. We become other people—people I don't even recognize."

Someday we may reach a level of spiritual maturity that allows us to be around *anyone* and still maintain our peacefulness and sense of self. But until then, we can help ourselves find and maintain our inner peace and serenity by avoiding negative people and making an effort to be around those who are more pleasant and peaceful, and who bring out our better qualities. This may be difficult or even impossible to do if the negative people in our lives are bosses, co-workers, family members, or others we feel obligated to be around, at least some of the time.

We can stay away from others who affect us adversely without being angry or judgmental about it. We can simply choose to spend our time elsewhere. We can stop seeing people who have a negative effect on us permanently, temporarily, or we can visit them infrequently and always on our own terms—no alcohol, for example. We can carefully choose the people we invite into our homes and avoid places where we know negative people will be.

We can make an effort to shop in places where the workers provide pleasant service. Even if it costs a little more or is a little out of our way, isn't it worth it to get a smile and a little friendly acknowledgment of our humanity? A rude, hostile salesclerk can ruin our day. Unless we know we can let it go and be unaffected, we can avoid such places and find better atmospheres in which to shop.

When we do all we can to avoid negative people, we can gain the needed break to step back and accept them as they are. We can give up trying to argue with them, reason with them, attack them, or defend ourselves against them. We can simply accept them for who they are, wish them well, and get on with taking care of ourselves. We can choose not to associate with the most negative aspects of other people's egos.

The other side of dealing with other people is cultivating relationships with those who bring out the best in us. Teachers, co-workers, friends, and family members who make an effort to respect, understand, encourage, and accept us can provide needed spiritual nourishment for us. They listen to us without a lot of assumptions and prejudices, and treat us respectfully, even when they don't agree with us. Just being around them seems to improve our outlook and self-image.

We can attract and encourage positive, pleasant, friendly, peaceful, happy interactions with others by behaving that way ourselves. We can't go around attacking people with our words or a sour facial expression, and expect them to treat us kindly. When we allow our spirits to come to the surface and express themselves, we are always peaceful and kind. We understand other people's fears and doubts, and overlook them. We accept people as they are, and bring out the best in them through patience, serenity, peacefulness, and joy.

Atmospheric Conditions

We can find and create atmospheres that are peaceful, loving, and conducive to our true inner happiness and well-being. We can examine the conditions that we can change in our environments and consciously choose where we spend our time. We can accept the conditions we can't change, and let go of struggling with negative people. We can discover the effects of our own attitudes and behaviors on the atmospheres in which we find ourselves, and learn to make a positive contribution. We can carry with us our own atmosphere of love, peace, gentleness, and joy, wherever we go.

As we grow and evolve on our own spiritual journey, we may find our tastes changing without any effort on our part. Various colors or styles of clothing, furniture, and architecture may appeal to us at various times in our lives. Our tastes in music and other art forms may change continually as we grow older.

We don't have to judge ourselves or others for these changing tastes. They aren't "good" or "bad"—they each serve their different purposes for different times in our lives. Now is the time to examine all these aspects of our environments, discover which ones contribute the most to our peace and happiness, and use that information in the best way. Our peace and happiness don't have to be strained by unpleasant environments. We can accept what we can't control and change what we can. It can even be great fun.

Exercises

Exercise One

Sounds. Identify the sounds in your environment that are pleasant, soothing, and peaceful to you. Which sounds are irritating, loud, or unpleasant in some way? What can you do about changing or eliminating them? Make the changes you need to make for your best sound atmospheres.

Exercise Two

Sights. Is there a place where you feel peaceful and happy? How often do you go there? Are there any pleasant natural environments that you visit regularly?

How can you schedule regular visits to your "bliss stations?" How can you improve your current environments visually to enhance your inner peace and happiness?

Exercise Three

Scents. Notice the scents in all of your environments. What are your favorites? How do they make you feel? How can you get more of them into your daily environments? Discover new scents by visiting bakeries, conservatories, or any other place you think might smell good to you. Bake your own breads and pies if those smells appeal to you. Explore other scents and surround yourself with your favorites.

CHAPTER TWELVE

Positive Choices

Have you really considered how many opportunities you have had to gladden yourself, and how many of them you have refused?

—A Course in Miracles

While we all have egos to contend with, there are many ways that we can remind ourselves to look at things in a new way, lead ourselves to our spirit's viewpoint, set ourselves up for spiritual experiences, and choose happiness. But we can't take advantage of these opportunities if we refuse to see or believe in them.

When Rachel was going through a long period of unhappiness, she experienced a recurring dream. "It was the only time in my life when I ever had the exact same dream over and over again," she says. "It started out very pleasantly. I was alone in my car, driving along a country road. The weather was gorgeous, and the wind whipped through my hair as I drove past the open fields. A huge orange sun was just beginning to set in the distance on my left." Rachel says this part of her dream felt peaceful and happy.

"As I drove along feeling great," Rachel continues, "I came to a little railroad crossing. There was no light or bell or anything like that—it was just one of those stop

215

signs you see on country roads. I came to a stop, looked down the tracks, and started across. But just as I got right smack on the train tracks, my car stalled. I tried turning the key in the ignition, but it wouldn't start up again. Then I noticed the faint rumbling of a train far off in the distance on my left. The sun was blinding me, so I couldn't see it, but I could feel it getting closer and closer. I kept pumping the gas pedal and turning the ignition key, but the car wouldn't respond. The rumbling of the train kept getting louder and louder. I felt panic rising in me as I feverishly tried to get the engine to turn over. This went on and on for what seemed like forever. Finally, the big dark silhouette of the train loomed closer and closer, the rumbling became deafeningly loud, and *bang!*—I got hit. That's when I woke up."

Rachel says she had this dream three or four times before she realized that *it never even occurred to her to get out of the car*—and even then, she only thought of it after she was awake. She says, "It was like this great lightning-bolt revelation when it finally hit me—*why don't I just get out of the car?* It was so simple and so *obvious,* but it had really never occurred to me before. I knew that dream was trying to tell me something about my life. My subconscious or spirit or whatever you want to call it was giving me an important message."

This story clearly illustrates how blind we can sometimes be to all the choices that are available to us. Things we think are impossible to eliminate from our lives may be easily left behind as we open up to growing in new ways. Things we think are impossible to achieve or incorporate into our lives may be readily available, if only we let ourselves believe it. All we have to do is *get out of the car.*

Habits

I believe that one of the main reasons we continue doing things we know aren't good for us, and not doing things that enhance our peace, joy, and well-being, is simply *habit*. Doing familiar things in familiar ways feels comfortable. Doing new things in new ways may feel strange and provoke our ego's fearfulness.

Because of the way our brain functions, this is normal. Patterns of behavior are recorded in our brain and feel second nature to us whenever we repeat them. New behaviors require the brain to create new patterns. It takes time and frequent repetition to form a new habit, but it can be done. And it's worth the time and effort to replace old, negative, self-defeating habits with new, positive ones.

We maintain habits of thought as well as behavior. The things we think about and the ways we think about them are old habits formed throughout our lives. Reminding ourselves that there is always another way to look at anything is the beginning of freeing ourselves from these old thought habits. Our habitual attitudes and beliefs affect our behavior, so we must examine them if we are to replace old behaviors with new ones.

Letting go of old habitual thoughts and behaviors becomes easier when we have an idea of what we want to replace them with. I believe that focusing on the positive choices we can make is much more effective than just trying to avoid negative ones. We can use many simple reminders to keep ourselves focused on a more positive outlook, resulting in more positive behaviors.

Keep It Simple

We humans don't seem to like doing what's difficult. Whenever possible, we tend to choose the easier way.

The things we enjoy most are usually those that come to us most easily. Since we know this about ourselves, we can set ourselves up for success by creating change in the easiest ways possible. We can create positive changes one small step at a time. We can choose methods of learning and growing that make use of our abilities and interests. We can get rid of old, unwanted habits by developing new ones.

Change takes time and effort, but we can make the process easier on ourselves in simple ways. Consistency and repetition are helpful. We can remember to take responsibility for our environments and daily schedules. We can take care of ourselves physically, emotionally, mentally, and spiritually. We can examine our patterns of thought and behavior pragmatically, letting go of any that do not enhance our true well-being and happiness.

As we let go of negative habits and replace them with positive ones, we can remember to focus on consistency and harmony between our mind, body, and spirit. Balance in these areas will result in our overall well-being and ability to contribute positively in the world. Simply being aware of these parts of ourselves can help us make the best choices for us. On a daily basis, we can remember to focus on the present and make time for relaxation, meditation, prayer, and recreation. We can fill our environments with positive sights, sounds, and scents. We can use affirmations and slogans to pull our minds back to our spirit's positive viewpoint.

Slogans

Remember in grade school when you did something wrong and your teacher made you write one hundred times that you wouldn't do it again? That teacher had the right idea about repeated phrases becoming fixed in our brain. But his or her mistake was in the negative wording of these assignments. *Always use positive wording in your slogans and affirmations.* For example, "I am relaxed and confident" is likely to have far better results than "I don't worry anymore." Many phrases are already recorded in our brains and play over and over, affecting our outlook and behavior; choosing positive slogans is simply taking responsibility for these recorded messages.

Slogans are affirmations of certain viewpoints and ideas. We can use them as quick, simple reminders to stay focused on or return to positive thoughts. We can repeat them over and over as *mantras,* or affirmations, to create new thought patterns in our minds, and replace old, negative ones. We all talk to ourselves in our minds all the time. We wake up in the morning and immediately start thinking. Why not make an effort to start the day with positive thoughts? It might just help us to feel a little more hopeful and happy. In any case, it couldn't hurt.

Members of Alcoholics Anonymous use such slogans as One Day at a Time, Easy Does It, Let Go and Let God, and Keep It Simple to help them remember the goals and tenets of their program. We can use slogans and affirmations in the same way. We can write, think, sing, or chant them repeatedly. We can make some little signs to put around our house or place of work to remind us of them. We can use the AA slogans, other common catch-phrases or prayer quotes, or we can make up our own.

"Be Here Now"
This simple phrase can be used to remind us to focus on the present moment, letting go of anxiety over the

past or the future. It can help us catch ourselves whenever we react to the present as if it were the past. It can help us maintain our focus on the present relationship or situation, and let go of past hurts, disappointments, frustrations, and anger.

Memory is a vital function of the human brain. But remembering is different from reliving—it involves a degree of detachment and perspective. When we dredge up old feelings from the past, we are not remembering. We're transferring those reactions to the present—and they don't belong here.

"Life Is Life"

No one can argue the truth of this statement. It's a variation on "Life goes on" and "Que sera, sera." But it's focused on the present, on what *is,* not what will be. This simple statement can remind us that life is full of unexpected changes, disappointments, and failures. It can shift our perspective to one of detachment and acceptance.

This slogan can clear out the delusions of control that can creep into our thinking, and help us let go of things we can't change. Life, after all, is life—all our worrying, anger, and manipulation can't control it. With an attitude of acceptance of life as it is, we can concentrate on what we *can* do something about—ourselves. We can choose our actions rationally and calmly when we've moved past our initial ego-reactions to whatever life sends us.

"Big Deal"

This can be expressed in many ways: *Who cares? So what? Let it go. Don't sweat the small stuff. Is this really important?* These phrases help us to keep things in proportion. After our egos initially react to minor problems as if they were major catastrophes, we can remind ourselves to calm down and begin examining the situation more realistically. We can ask ourselves what the problem really is, what the results might be, and why we reacted to it so strongly. Then we can take a calm, rational approach to solving or accepting it.

"It's the principle of the thing" has become a cliche justification for fighting it out to the bitter end. If it's not important, it's not important. The "big deal" is usually just our ego kicking up. We can learn to recognize what doesn't really matter. We can let it go, give it up, and be peaceful.

* * * * *

Slogans and affirmations can help us control our reactions, feelings, and thoughts. They can be useful tools in maintaining our serenity and peacefulness. They can be just one small part of taking responsibility for ourselves and our happiness.

The Power of Thought

Slogans can be one helpful tool in bringing our minds back to a positive viewpoint when we find ourselves slipping into old, negative beliefs and attitudes. But there are many other ways we can choose to think about positive things in positive ways. We can always return to a pragmatic examination of our old habits to discover what thoughts and behaviors contribute to negative and positive viewpoints.

The Hindu *Upanishads,* the Buddhist *Dharmapada,* and the Judeo-Christian *Bible* all tell us of the power of thought. We are reminded over and over to take care in choosing our thoughts. But often, we assume that all the things that go on in our minds are beyond our control. We believe that the input coming from outside of us is uncontrollable and unavoidable. We think of our thoughts as welcome or unwelcome outsiders roaming around freely in our minds.

The truth is, we do have control over our thoughts and much of the stimulus that enters our minds. In the chapter on atmospheres, I talked about such aspects of our environments as sounds, colors, smells, and greenery. But there are many other sources of input for our minds. What do we choose to read? What television programs do we watch? What do we think about?

In this day of health consciousness, we are careful about the things we put into our bodies. We watch our consumption of fat, calories, cholesterol, salt, sugars, nicotine, caffeine, alcohol and other drugs, and dangerous food additives and pollutants in our air and water. Shouldn't we be at least as careful about what goes into our minds? If true peace of mind and happiness are our goals, we must at least think about these questions: What are we allowing into our minds every day? What effects are these things having on our peace, tranquility, and joyfulness?

Hugh Prather writes, "You cannot realistically expect your mind to function on a level higher than the level of ideas you continuously feed it." What kind of diet are you feeding your mind? What ideas do you allow into your consciousness every day? What can you do about limiting the negatives and increasing the positives? We can remember that much of the input our mind receives results from our habits—of reading, watching television, listening to the radio, tapes, or records, and talking and listening to people. All of these choices are within our control.

When we examine these choices pragmatically, we can ask ourselves what effects each of them has on our state of mind, emotions, peace, and happiness. Does reading romantic novels make you feel disappointed in real life? Does talking with certain people leave you feeling resentful, angry, inferior, or hopeless? Does watching the news make you fearful, angry, or depressed?

Let's pragmatically examine all the things with which we fill our minds. Being informed about all kinds of things that we can't do anything about or that make us fearful, anxious, or worried only clutters up our mind and prevents us from focusing our time and energy on the positive things we *can* do.

Entertainment

We don't have to limit ourselves to "educational" reading, movies, television, or music. Pure entertainment is valuable. We all need recreation, humor, and relaxation. But we can learn to be sensitive to the negative effects any kind of art or entertainment may have on us, and eliminate it from our lives. It's important to remember that we *can* avoid most of the negative input we allow into our minds.

Positive entertainment makes us feel good—happy, hopeful, inspired, encouraged, relaxed, and peaceful. Do we really need some "expert" to tell us that watching senseless gore and sick fantasies of people being cruel to each other is not going to have positive effects on our outlook? We can have enough self-respect to guard the door to our minds more carefully. Entertainment should help you, not harm your peace and happiness.

Soul Food

We can nourish and nurture our hearts, spirits, souls, or highest selves in many ways. In his book, *Super Joy,* Paul Pearsall calls this "spiritual nutrition" or "soul food." This kind of self-care begins with caring for our bodies. When we are feeling well physically, we are better able to focus our attention on other things. If we allow ourselves to become run-down, we may feel we just can't cope when something happens demanding our attention.

Taking responsibility for our health and fitness can also lead us to spend our time in enjoyable ways. Sports and other forms of exercise can be opportunities for pleasant social interaction with other people. Taking care of our bodies as well as our appearance can also help us feel self-confident.

We take care of our bodies in healthy ways by eating properly, getting enough enjoyable exercise and plenty of rest, and giving up any substances that have a negative effect on us—such as sugar, caffeine, alcohol, and nicotine. Doing what's good for us and giving up what's not good for us isn't self-sacrifice—it's self-care and self-love.

Prayer and Meditation

When we create our daily schedules, it's important to make time for many different activities: work, recreation, family and other relationships, physical self-care, and time with nature. It's also important to set aside time in every day for prayer and meditation. Even if we don't believe in praying to a father/God figure in the traditional sense, the act of prayer helps us focus our thoughts and return to our spiritual viewpoint.

At the beginning of every day is a good time for a prayer ritual. This doesn't require any special religious belief or act, it simply means we set aside time at the start of our day to think about our highest goals, ideals, and beliefs. We get our attitudes centered in our spiritual viewpoint and ask for guidance and help—from God, our Higher Power, or our own spirits. We set ourselves up for making wise decisions and harmless, helpful, loving contributions wherever we go.

Meditation doesn't necessarily mean visualizations, chants, or anything special other than taking time to let go of all our ego-centered thoughts for a while. We can let ourselves drift in a relaxed, peaceful state of mind, or we can focus on a question or problem, opening our minds to possible solutions and other ways of looking at it. It's important to take time for prayer and meditation every day, no matter how we do it. It helps us to spend a few minutes, on a regular basis, opening our minds and relaxing our egos.

Learning

One of the most enjoyable ways we can feed our spirit is through the process of learning. No matter how old we are or how long it's been since we left school, we can all continue learning throughout our lives. We can learn through books, classes, or travel. We can study another culture or language, take up a musical instrument, or read a book on a subject that's new to us. We can learn how to play golf or tennis or ride a horse. We can learn to cook a souffle or plaster a wall.

There is no limit to all the new things we can learn. We can learn new skills and ideas every day of our lives. Spending our time in this way not only keeps our minds working and builds our self-confidence, but it also feeds our spiritual need for growth and expansion. It keeps our minds and hearts alive.

Caring for Living Things

We have talked about surrounding ourselves with living things from the viewpoint of creating positive atmospheres. But there is another reason for filling our lives with plants and animals: having them around gives us the activity of nurturing. This kind of activity is a gift for us as well as the plants or animals we care for. Taking care of other living things—helping them live, grow, and flourish—gives as much to us as it does to them.

We all need to share our spiritual energy, to encourage, strengthen, nourish, and help other living things. We can surround ourselves with potted plants, outdoor gardens or window boxes, and pets. We can do volunteer work for the Humane Society or feed the birds outside. We can water a sapling or plant an acorn. We can care for the whole earth by conserving water and energy, recycling, using biodegradable products, reusing plastic containers rather than discarding them, and disposing of toxic substances properly. We can each contribute positively to the whole of life—of which we are an inseparable part.

Present Moment Living

Each present moment offers us something to experience and is full of potential. Some of these moments slip by unnoticed while we worry, fear, doubt, and resent the realities of life. We often look back regretfully at all the lost opportunities for love, joy, and sharing. As we are becoming aware of all the negatives we can eliminate from our lives and environments, we can also become aware of each beautiful moment as it occurs.

When we let go of fretting over past regrets and future fantasies, we can wake up to the moment at hand. We can become aware of the touch, the smile, the gentle presence of love, peace, joy, and beauty all around us. We can become appreciative of each special moment as it comes. We can stop missing all the wonderful opportunities we have for joy. We can nourish our souls on the potential peace in every present moment.

Open-Mindedness

Having an open mind is one of the most important gifts we can give our spirits. When our minds are clogged up with assumptions, prejudices, and expectations, there is no room for peace, love, and truth. We can't receive all the nourishment our spirit longs for when the door to our mind is closed. We can't recognize and accept what our spirits need and what will bring us true inner peace and happiness unless we're open to it.

Open-mindedness means letting go of all our assumptions about ourselves, others, and life. It means giving up our ego's grievances and defenses against others. It means forgiveness, tolerance, acceptance, and willingness to learn. It means realizing that there is always another way to look at anything. This is the beginning of understanding ourselves and others, recognizing our spirits, and choosing a loving, happy viewpoint.

Spiritual Care for Difficult Times

There are times when we face difficulties and feel overwhelmed. There are times when we just seem to feel "blue" for no apparent reason. There are times when the realities of this world get us down. These times happen to *everyone,* but there are many ways we can help ourselves through them. We can take the actions that help lead us back to serenity, tranquility, acceptance, equanimity, peace, love, and true happiness.

Each of us can identify specific activities and sur-roundings that best contribute to our recovery from temporary depression. The following is a list of things many people find helpful:

- music
- talking it over with another person
- thinking it through
- accepting it and letting it run its course
- reading inspirational, uplifting literature
- writing in a journal
- gratitude
- humor
- helping others
- going to special places
- taking a bath
- physical work or exercise

Music

One man says, "Usually, when I'm depressed, I listen to very depressing music at first. I really go for it. It's like this music understands the way I feel, it really knows me, and it's depressed right along with me. It's almost like having someone there to share my depres-sion with. And it's someone who's perfect, because they've written poetry for me and tunes that speak to my mood. Then, when I've had enough of depression and I need to transcend into a more uplifting tempo, I'll try to make a transition by playing music that's more and more uplifting."

One woman says any music that's very "spirited" makes her feel better. "Some music will just change my mood if I listen to it long enough—reggae, Cajun, certain kinds of rock. Anything really lively and upbeat." Another woman says she plays very soft, peaceful music and calm, uplifting meditation tapes when she feels down. "I find this music very healing for me," she says. We can experiment with different kinds of music to determine which ones work best for us under various circumstances. We can accept the gift of music and use its healing power.

Talking with Others

Many people find that talking with others helps them express and clarify their feelings, vent frustration, feel understood, and get past a period of depression. One woman says, "I share my depression so I don't have to carry it alone." A man says, "I get someone else's viewpoint on the situation and my feelings so that I'm not all alone with it in myself."

When we share our thoughts and feelings with others, we can discover that we are not so alone as we may have thought. We can look at our thoughts and feelings in new ways when we put them out there for others to see and discuss. We can find new intimacy and love with others who are willing to listen and try to understand us.

We can talk our feelings over with a family member, friend, therapist, clergyperson, or doctor. We can find safe places to discuss our feelings in support group meetings. We can diffuse simmering feelings by airing them out. In the light of day, our worries, fears, and sorrow may not seem so dark.

Thinking It Through or Accepting It

Some people say a great deal of thought and self-examination helps them sort out their feelings and understand circumstances, situations, and relationships better. One man says, "I pull it apart as much as I possibly can, examine the elements and the reasons why, and where my feelings come from. I break things down so that I can understand some of the steps that lead up to the depression. If I know that I have done what I can to understand the circumstances, then I feel much more comfortable in either trying to change the circumstances or resigning myself to them. Then I can allow the depression to live its life as quickly as possible and be gone."

But other people have found that accepting the feelings without analyzing them too much works better. A woman says, "I don't sit around and try to figure out why I'm depressed anymore. I just accept it—and that takes away a lot of its power." Another says, "I just know now that it'll pass. I can think myself out of it, because I know from past experience that it's not the end of the world and I'll be all right."

Gratitude

We've all heard that every dark cloud has a silver lining and we should look on the bright side and count our blessings. But sometimes these encouraging words seem hollow and meaningless. Sometimes we may feel completely unable to see anything good about our situation or circumstance. Sometimes we may feel we have no blessings to count at all.

These are the times when gratitude often works best. One woman says all she has to do to let go of a low mood is to "sit back, remember where I was five years ago, and get thankful." Looking around for the tiniest things to be grateful for can help us see all the wonderful blessings we've taken for granted. Looking back at our growth and development over the years can make us realize just how far we've come and give us hope for how much further we can go from here. There is no one in the world, at any time in their life, who really has nothing for which to be grateful.

Other Gifts to Ourselves

As shown by the previous list, there are many other ways we can help ourselves out of low or difficult periods. We can read inspiring, uplifting literature; take "time out" to pamper ourselves or just relax; keep busy with activities that help others or provide constructive results, such as gardening, cleaning, cooking, or craft projects. We can sing, dance, run, walk, swim, bike, or play ball to get our blood circulating and our brain's natural stress-relievers activated. We can spend time in our favorite places, surround ourselves with our favorite things, and write our thoughts and feelings in a journal. We can help ourselves to all the wonderful gifts that are available to us in the world and in ourselves.

Experiencing Our Spirituality

Spiritual experience is personal and individual. We can't get it by just going to a church, or doing good works, or saying a prescribed number of prayers. We can't create transformational spiritual experiences by sheer will, but we can encourage them by being open to them, recognizing them, accepting them, and paying attention to what they can teach us.

Experiencing our spirituality simply means being aware of it, being there with it. Sometimes this happens just for a brief moment, but even then we know something special has happened. We may ignore it, attribute it to some superficial condition, or even feel afraid of it. But if we want to open our minds to our spirituality, if we are ready to experience it, it's there for us.

All the things we've talked about in this book can help set us up for spiritual experiences. When we let go of our ego's viewpoint, even for a moment, we open ourselves up to the knowledge of our spirit. Prayer and meditation help many people relax away from their ego's viewpoint and open up to their spirits. But an awareness and sensitivity to the spiritual aspect of every experience, relationship, encounter, and event can also help us see everything from our spirit's viewpoint.

Spiritual experiences aren't always spectacular visions or lightning-bolt revelations. Sometimes they're subtle, quiet, and brief. Sometimes they sneak up on us when we least expect it. Sometimes they're misinterpreted. They can be as simple as a smile, or as complex as a scientific breakthrough. They're everywhere, all the time. We just have to open our eyes and our hearts to their presence.

Positive Choices

We don't analyze and adjust to outer circumstances of our lives to create happiness. We simply help ourselves to remember our center, our spirit, and our source of happiness by keeping distractions to it to a minimum. We examine every choice we make pragmatically to see if it enhances or damages our true inner peace, well-being, and happiness.

Throughout this book, I have talked a lot about being pragmatic, about examining our beliefs, attitudes, and behaviors to determine what works for us. *A Course in Miracles* says, "'The good is what works' is a sound though insufficient statement. Only the good *can* work. Nothing else works at all." We've wasted enough time and energy on what will never make us truly happy. Now let's stick with what works, and let's abandon what does not work, no matter how logical it may seem or how much we wish it would work.

If our beliefs, attitudes, and actions cause no one any harm, and help us to live fuller, healthier, saner, truly happier lives, what else do we need to know about them? In the movie, *Crimes and Misdemeanors,* an elderly patriarch of a Jewish family contends that even if it turns out that his beliefs are wrong—that there is no God, no afterlife, and no cosmic justice—*he will have lived a better life for having believed and acted as if there were.* Let's hang on to those beliefs that work for our highest well-being, while allowing ourselves to grow and evolve.

Since we have the choice, why waste it agonizing over the past and worrying about the future? Why waste time and energy wishing the things we can't change were different? Why ignore all the chances we have to change the things we can? Go ahead—dare to be optimistic. Dare to be truly happy. What have you got to lose? Being a Pollyanna couldn't possibly be any worse than being a Scrooge. Give it a try and see what happens.

Exercises

Exercise One

Slogans. Choose a slogan that feels powerful for you, one you think you need to work on. Let this slogan be your theme for a week. Write it on cards and put the cards in your pockets, purse, dresser drawers, on your mirrors, in your car, and anyplace else where they will be in your sight for the whole week. Begin every morning by repeating the slogan over and over while you shower, shave, or dress. Take a moment to repeat the slogan a few times throughout the day. Before going to sleep, repeat the slogan over and over in your mind.

Exercise Two

Guard Your Mind. Pay attention to all the input you allow into your mind—television, radio, reading material, other people, and all the other sources of information that bombard you daily. Which ones can you avoid? Which ones have a positive effect on your outlook, feelings, attitudes, and happiness? How can you reduce the negatives and increase the positives?

Exercise Three

Soul Food. Think of all the ways in which you nourish your highest spiritual self. How many other ways could you contribute positively to your own mental, physical, emotional, and spiritual self-care? What choices can you make for helping yourself out of low moods? What kinds of gifts can you give yourself all the time?

Equanimity

Growth is always a gradual process, a bridge slowly crossed and not a corner sharply turned.

—John Powell

We often talk about spiritual experiences or turning points as "rebirths" or "new beginnings," but really view them as graduations. We think, *Whew! Thank goodness that part of my life is over!* We forget that rebirth means a new infancy, new lessons to learn and growth to experience. Life is never free of challenges, difficulties, or pain. But we can change our responses to these realities of life, and therein lies our spiritual maturity or equanimity.

People say they feel "smarter," "more aware," and "more accepting" as they grow through their spiritual evolution. They still face the same problems, but they "perceive things differently." William James listed the following effects of spiritual experiences:

- a firm belief in and trust in a Higher Power

- a feeling of freedom

- a shifting of energy toward loving others

- patience, tolerance, and gentleness

- loss of fears and anxieties
- peacefulness, no matter what happens
- living in the present moment
- moral consistency; behavior reflecting highest ideals
- acceptance of imperfection
- simplicity
- optimism
- detachment; loss of dependencies

These are the results, rewards, and evidence of growing closer to our spiritual selves. They don't happen overnight, and they don't mean the end of making choices. But choosing to see through the eyes of our loving spirit rather than our fearful ego is no sacrifice—it's liberation. Freedom from our self-imposed prison of fear, doubt, anger, worry, and sorrow is its own reward.

When we learn to grant ourselves this freedom, we become able to help others. There is no split between doing good for others and for ourselves. If we are truly doing what is good for others, it will have good effects for us; if we are truly doing what is good for us, others will benefit. Our individual peace and serenity may not save the world, but it couldn't hurt. One more person walking around with a loving attitude can only make the world that much better.

Equanimity lives inside each of us right now. It waits quietly and peacefully while we sleepwalk through our conditional lives. Let's wake up to our potential for good. Let's look inward and really see ourselves. Let's look outward and really see the world around us. Let's wake up to the incomparable joy of living unconditionally.

BIBLIOGRAPHY
AND SUGGESTED READING

Allen, James. *As A Man Thinketh*. New York: Putnam, 1959.

Beattie, Melody. *Beyond Codependency: And Getting Better All the Time*. Center City, Minn.: Hazelden Educational Materials, 1989.

Buscaglia, Leo. *Bus 9 to Paradise*. New York: Ballentine, 1987.

Campbell, Joseph, with Bill Moyers. *The Power of Myth*. New York: Doubleday, 1988.

Cleveland, Martha. *The Twelve Step Response to Chronic Illness and Disability*. Center City, Minn.: Hazelden Educational Materials, 1988.

Collins, Vincent P. *Acceptance*. St. Meinrad, Ind.: Abbey Press, 1960.

Foundation for Inner Peace. *A Course in Miracles*. Tiburon, Calif.: Foundation for Inner Peace, 1976.

Hirshfield, Gerald. *My Ego, My Higher Power, and I*. Van Nuys, Calif.: HI Productions, 1985.

James, William. *The Varieties of Religious Experience*. New York: Penguin Classics, 1982.

Jampolsky, Gerald. *Goodbye to Guilt*. New York: Bantam Books, 1985.

Jampolsky, Gerald. *Out of Darkness Into the Light: A Journey of Inner Healing*. New York: Bantam Books, 1989.

Jordan, William George. *The Majesty of Calmness*. Center City, Minn.: Hazelden Educational Materials, 1980.

Kushner, Harold. *When All You've Ever Wanted Isn't Enough*. New York: Pocket Books, 1986.

Kushner, Harold. *When Bad Things Happen to Good People*. New York: Schocken Books, 1981.

Murphy, Joseph. *The Power of Your Subconscious Mind*. New York: Bantam Books, 1982.

Pearsall, Paul. *Superimmunity*. New York: McGraw-Hill, 1987.

Pearsall, Paul. *Super Joy*. New York: Doubleday, 1988.

Peck, M. Scott. *The Road Less Traveled: A New Psychology of Love, Traditional Values, and Spiritual Growth*. New York: Touchstone, 1978.

Phillips, J. B. *Your God Is Too Small*. New York: Macmillan, 1961.

Pitzele, Sefra Kobrin. *We Are Not Alone: Learning to Live with Chronic Illness*. New York: Workman Press, 1986.

Powell, John. *Happiness Is an Inside Job*. Valencia, Calif.: Tabor Publishing, 1989.

Prather, Hugh. *Notes on How to Live in the World . . . and Still Be Happy*. New York: Doubleday, 1986.

Prather, Hugh. *The Quiet Answer*. New York: Doubleday, 1982.

Radner, Gilda. *It's Always Something*. New York: Simon & Schuster, 1989.

Russell, A. J., ed. *God Calling*. New York: Jove Books, 1978.

Schwartz, Lynn Sharon. *Disturbances in the Field*. New York: Harper & Row, 1983.

Siegel, Bernie. *Peace, Love, & Healing*. New York: Harper & Row, 1989.

Stearns, Ann Kaiser. *Coming Back: Rebuilding Lives After Crisis and Loss*. New York: Ballentine, 1988.

Stearns, Ann Kaiser. *Living Through Personal Crisis*. New York: Ballentine, 1985.